Trade Promotion
Strategies Best Practices

Trade Promotion Strategies Best Practices

Michel Borgeon and Claude Cellich

First published in 2012 by Business Expert Press
Business Expert Press, LLC
222 East 46th Street, New York, NY 10017
www.businessexpertpress.com

ISBN-13: 978-160649-229-1 (paperback)
ISBN-13: 978-160649-230-7 (e-book)

DOI 10.4128/9781606492307

A publication in the Business Expert Press International Business collection

Collection ISSN: 1948-2752 (print)
Collection ISSN: 1948-2760 (electronic)

Cover design by Jonathan Pennell
Interior design by Scribe Inc.

First edition: January 2012

10 9 8 7 6 5 4 3 2 1

Printed in the United States of America.

Abstract

Globalization has revolutionized how trade is conducted. New opportunities have been created, coupled with higher risks and increased competition. Firms involved in international trade have had to adapt to a rapidly changing global environment to remain competitive. To assist export-oriented enterprises, particularly small and medium ones, national trade promotion organizations have developed innovative strategies and incentives. Strategic considerations in trade promotion are examined in part I, while the national trade promotion initiatives considered most effective have been selected and presented as cases in parts II and III. Throughout the book, readers are provided with the best available practices and explanations of how a select group of trade promotion organizations have become relevant partners to their export-oriented enterprises.

Keywords

Clients' satisfaction survey, competitiveness, exporter profile, export strategies, evaluation tools, fair trade, market analysis, online assistance, trade promotion budget, trade maps, trade promotion organisations, trade promotion strategies, trade representation, Australia, Canada, Mauritius, Taiwan, United States

Contents

Abbreviations

ASEAN	Association of Southeast Asian Nations
COMESA	Common Market for Eastern and Southern Africa
CRM	customer relationship management
FDI	foreign direct investment
GDP	gross domestic product
HS	harmonized system
ITC	International Trade Centre
MFN	most favored nation
NAFTA	North American Free Trade Association
NTIC	new technologies on information and communication
ROI	return on investment
SITC	standard international trade classification
SME	small and medium-sized enterprise
SWOT	strengths weaknesses opportunities threats
TPO	trade promotion organization
UNCTAD	United Nations Conference on Trade and Development
UNSO	United Nations Statistical Office
USAID	U.S. Agency for International Development
WTO	World Trade Organization

Preface

After years of involvement in trade development and export promotion with the International Trade Centre (ITC), particularly in the past decade, we have witnessed a significant shift from traditional promotion activities to innovative trade tools, instruments, and measures. As a result of increased globalization, the Internet revolution, and intense competition, national trade promotion organizations (TPOs) have been forced to restructure and reorient themselves to remain relevant to the business sector. These changes reflect the need to provide exporters with sophisticated tools and targeted counseling services to compete successfully in foreign markets. In view of the substantial investment required to mount export promotion programs, greater attention is being given to the development of appropriate performance and monitoring instruments to assess the return on investment (ROI) on trade promotion expenditures.

Throughout this book, we have highlighted the development of new export promotion strategies to enhance the export capabilities of firms, particularly small and medium-sized enterprises (SMEs), to face global competition. Another key issue is the need to focus on multiyear trade strategies while moving away from ad hoc or short-term programs without an adequate evaluation of previous export promotion initiatives. Successful execution of trade promotion strategies requires closer and sustained collaboration between the private sector and TPOs while being transparent, accountable, and responsible to all concerned stakeholders.

During our research, we have selected a number of national TPOs for their successful export promotion strategies, several of them recent recipients of the annual TPO Network Awards for their innovative approach. Trade instruments and information portals have been described in detail to enable their adoption by other TPOs committed to best practices.

In view of the limited information in this area, we have restricted our research to the best-known TPOs for their innovative and effective activities. Further research should be carried out in the near future as new tools and structures are being initiated. We trust that readers will find the information provided helpful and stimulate further research by scholars, trade officials, and business executives, thereby contributing to the grow-ing body of knowledge in the latest trade promotion strategies.

This book would not have been possible without our association with the ITC and TPOs in Africa, Asia, Europe, the Middle East, and the Americas. Our teaching at the International University in Geneva has further contributed to our research in identifying the best practices in export promotion strategies. A special thanks goes to Eric Willumsen for his support and encouragement throughout this project.

Introduction

Historical Background: Trade Promotion Has Always Been There

Even in ancient times, trade promotion was recognized as a key strategy, either at the national or the regional level. Trade fairs were known all over Europe in the Middle Ages and supported by local authorities. Phoenician traders were known throughout the whole Mediterranean area, and Venetian prosperity was based on strong national trade promotion policies from the fifteenth century. By the nineteenth century, many nations were involved in trade promotion strategies by engaging in overseas trade.

In short, trade promotion strategies have always been in the forefront as well as in the background of international relations. Traditionally, trade promotion was an extension of diplomatic strategies.

Closer to our times, trade expansion since the 1950s regularly outpaced domestic economic growth. With the influence of international trade organizations, notably the World Trade Organization (WTO), and regional organizations like the European Union (EU), the North American Free Trade Association (NAFTA), the Association of Southeast Asian Nations (ASEAN), and the Common Market for Eastern and Southern Africa (COMESA), the platform for trade negotiations has been extended to global issues, where trade promotion policies are implemented. Such trade record performances help to reinforce the conviction that export promotion is a major tool for trade development.

Trade Promotion: A More-Than-Ever Valid Tool in Hard Times

Recalling the economic and social events that unexpectedly questioned the international system since the 2008 world economic and financial crisis, followed by high volatility of the major economic indicators, it is clear that trade trends are difficult to predict with accuracy.

The erratic economic and social context in which the international system is thrust will probably remain for quite some time, with signs of deep structural changes emerging for both nations and civil society, government organizations and nongovernment organizations (NGOs). One example is the global climate, which faces extreme short-term variations in some regions and unexpected trends, causing quick and deep phenomena to emerge such as the following:

- Oil prices fluctuating sharply (not always linked to supply and demand), based on expected demand or available stocks
- Food crises (shortage of essential products with highly fluctuating and rising prices)
- Highly volatile primary commodity prices (gold, silver, palladium, platinum, rare earth minerals—essential for electronics, rubber, etc.) fueled by shifting demand, financial maneuvers, and/or speculation
- Unstable supply chains for many manufactures, always challenged by shifting production factors
- Currency fluctuations (hardly managed by central banks or monetary authorities) around the U.S. dollar or euro, which influence competitiveness for companies bound to one currency and, for example, could cause a small operating margin to become a deficit by a sudden "de facto" devaluation over a short period of 6 months or even 3 months

In this context, trade promotion strategies are quite a challenge to design, implement, and assess. Observing and drawing lessons from successful best practices are more important than ever.

Hard Times for Trade Promotion Strategies in a More Complex and Interdependent World

Recent trends in world trade, from sustained growth over decades to sudden and unpredicted deep crisis followed by fragile recoveries, tend to lead to the following consequences:

- Challenging traditional trade links

- Breaking established positions
- Moving in or out of supply chains

These happenings bring both opportunities and major problems in formulating consistent strategies in trade policies and promotion. More than ever, they have to be formulated within a dynamic international context and the constraints of the national environment (labor and social costs, sustainability, environmental issues, limited elasticity of factory costs, etc.).

Trade expansion has brought about increased interdependence among trading partners, with important implications for national trade promotion programs. Moreover, the impact of fluctuations of the major currencies more or less controlled (even if the issue of "competitive devaluation" has been condemned by the latest G20 meeting in 2011) can transform a marginal benefit into a net loss in less than 3 months for a major multinational (e.g., European Aeronautic Defence and Space [EADS]), as well as for medium-sized, export-oriented enterprises.

Within the World Trade Organization (WTO), concerted actions are now recognized as a key for avoiding domino effects in fragile postcrisis times, and trade promotion policies cannot be formulated independently from regional agreements (bilateral or multilateral). Sometimes, national protection is required by lobbyists even if they openly contradict agreements. This makes trade agreements more difficult to formulate, if not to apply, explaining why the Doha Round has yet to be concluded. The reality is that the national needs of the domestic environment (e.g., employment increase, trade deficit control, new industries incentives, visible or invisible sector subventions) frequently conflict with development in international trade, at least in a trade liberalization perspective.

World trade is now dominated by interdependence (i.e., globally linked). For instance, an automobile is now partially produced in a variety of countries, assembled in others, and then sold elsewhere (Ford in Europe, Renault and Nissan in Europe and Asia, Volkswagen in China, etc.). Such operations are clear demonstrations of comparative advantages dominating over manufacturing as well as trading across boundaries.

Michael Czinkota[1] has proposed an innovative analysis of three possible trading policy options to resolve conflicts of interest among parties, summarized as follows:

1. To reduce economic interdependence by controlling trade through trade restrictions. As a result, domestic economic would be maintained, but each individual country concerned by these restrictions and the world community would be deprived of the benefits gained by trade. A clear illustration of such a choice is Cuba's trade policy.

2. To share and control damage in trade. Nations would not only trade off trade liberalization measures against each other but also negotiate for trade liberalization against trade restrictions. For such an approach to be implemented, however, it would also require that those industries gaining from liberalization measures share these benefits with less fortunate industries suffering from the trade restrictive measures. It should be noted that trade restriction can consist in "shadow" measures like nonquantitative standards and norms, safety or health regulations, environment requirements, and so on, including all denominated "nontariff barriers." The game can be played along supply chain agreements within the trading partners

3. To bring about "reasonably free" trade. Market demand would be accepted as the primary engine of trade activities with the minimum of distortion through policy measures. Such an approach requires close cooperation in wide areas like harmonization of monetary policies, increase in the transparency of domestic economic policies, and opening up of trade flows for firms rather than products. This approach is illustrated by the Doha Round discussions, but with limited results to date, as long as a significant number of countries prefer to keep the previously mentioned policy options, even not openly.

It is essential to consider that with the increased global competition, national strategies and decisions have become more rather than less important, questioning the fundamentals of liberal analysis. Even if companies are the final key actors, they need to benefit from the best possible environment at the national level. They are under pressure and challenges, with strong domestic rivals, competitive home-based suppliers, and ever more demanding local customers, including growing overseas markets requirements forcing them to innovate constantly. Companies have to deploy their resources in a forward-looking, dynamic, and challenging national environment within established and predictable rules, supported by trade promotion organizations (TPOs) who definitely play a dominant role.

These considerations imply that studying trade promotion strategies and the parties concerned (governments as well as the business sector) is a key issue. This is reviewed in the following chapter.

PART I

Trade Promotion Principles and Review of Key Strategic Functions

CHAPTER 1

Why Develop Trade Promotion Strategies, and Who Is Concerned?*

For all trade parties concerned, public or private, one key fact governs the national and international landscape: Progressive liberalization of markets with the consequent globalization of world trade. As a result, local firms as well as governments are likely to face increased competition at home as well as in the international market place, with diminishing possibilities to protect their country's economy and their businesses from outside challenges.

Now more than ever, the competitive advantages that any firm or country has achieved are becoming smaller and less durable. At the international level, executives are therefore facing several strategic challenges:

- Becoming globally competitive (or at least improving their ability to do so)
- Pursuing new business opportunities (in line with market liberalization)
- Maintaining their business as usual based on the perception that, for the time being, they still enjoy comparative advantages or national protection, with inevitably diminishing sales and/or profit

---

*This chapter has been inspired and adapted from conclusions drawn after a symposium organized by the International Trade Centre (ITC), entitled "Executive Forum on National Export Strategies," at the third World Conference of Trade Promotion Organizations in Marrakech, Morocco (October 25–27, 2000). The symposium findings have been summarized and reproduced in the ITC publication, *Redefining Trade Promotion: The Need for a Strategic Response* (out of print).

At the national level, the long-term implications are also significant. The country—more specifically, the government—has to establish and maintain a favorable business environment in an increased global competition, where best national practices are copied promptly if they are found replicable (e.g., the success of free trade zone areas).

Such a trade environment should

- encourage local entrepreneurs to invest in new technologies, markets, and products or services (home or abroad);
- help increase employment (local or indirectly through outsourcing);
- generate specialized skills (adapting and skill training);
- help generate innovation and new technologies in order to maintain and increase competitive advantages (as is the case in China over the past decade); and
- ultimately generate profits (fairly taxed, with proper incentives to reinvest "at home").

If the previous points are not taken into account, the business sector will inevitably suffer, gradually losing market shares abroad as well as in the domestic market. It should be noted that this affects small and medium-sized enterprises (SMEs) and multinational corporations, with greater concern for SMEs.

This is a particularly challenging scenario for the public-sector planner and strategy maker in a developing or transition economy. In such economies, the private sector may be vulnerable, with more day-to-day survival concerns than long-term development considerations, making these economies unprepared and unable to take any kind of leadership role in response to the requirements of new global competition.

Therefore the national challenge consists of formulating and managing a national export strategy that is effective and can be implemented by all concerned parties. Establishing an export strategy requires addressing the following:

- How to proceed in the national context
- How to identify and apply success principles
- How to benefit from best practices examples

From a "mission statement" point of view, the following key areas should also be considered:

- What should a national export development strategy (NEDS) encompass in the dynamics of today's international markets?
- To what extent should it focus on market development, improving traditional promotional instruments—such as trade fair participation—trade missions, and commercial representation services in foreign markets?
- Can it identify new avenues, even nontraditional ones, as some successful countries/exporting industries are testing and implementing (e.g., South Korea, Mauritius, and some strategic sectors in India)?

Once the idea of defining a national trade promotion strategy is adopted, the next step has to consider the following issues:

- Identify key principles.
- Analyze examples of best practices.

A National Export Development Strategy (NEDS) gives priority to market development and improved traditional promotional instruments. It may also concentrate on the delivery of more efficient public-sector services addressing the obstacles found in new or nontraditional markets, overriding the difficulties met by enterprises considering exports. Such difficulties may involve collecting and purchasing trade-related information, covering initial market contacts and other research costs. These difficulties, if not overcome, lead to a kind of self-limitation to invest in new opportunities, preferring well-established traditional networks with known consequences on the company's competitiveness.

A NEDS may mix promotional initiatives, both traditional and nontraditional, organized on behalf of existing enterprises, with on-profile supporting programs. Such programs would be designed to generate new export capacities rather than to strengthen existing links.

The starting point would be, of course, to assume that there is a need for the local business community to come close to international standards of competitiveness, which could be considered as a subjective rather than an objective process. Such initiatives consist of setting up an expanded export strategy to address all the factors reducing the cost of the export transaction by

- improving forward and backward linkages within and among local industries and, to some extent, integrating the production process, generating higher value-added production capacities (i.e., an assessment of the value-added chain to address the weaker points);
- helping the companies involved in the value chain acquire new technologies;
- building new, export-oriented competencies for these value chains.

However, to be effective, such a process must be integrated into the overall economic-planning framework. This has a clear implication: It should not simply deal with one-time foreign market development and promotion but establish a national competitiveness framework, creating an export culture and national consensus, thereby developing new export industries. There are many cases of new exporting industries showing such development strategies in developing countries or economies in transition in specific sectors, like apparel in Sri Lanka, cotton manufactures in Egypt, software industries in India, and high-quality branded wine in Chile and South Africa. Each of these export sectors should be screened to reveal the underlying building process.

Of course, this building process implies a clear policy statement: Such a choice is obvious for small or limited-resource countries (e.g., Singapore, Sri Lanka) but not so for the larger ones (e.g., Brazil, Indonesia, United States), for which exports represent a less significant share of gross domestic product (GDP). In short, the export strategy should address the issue of present and future international competitiveness throughout the country's supply chain.

This leads to the conclusion that two of the most important factors need to be reassessed in the process of managing an export development strategy:

- The direct and substantive involvement of all relevant parties beyond the private sector, namely ministries con-cerned with strategy-management processes and building

infrastructures—industry, agriculture, public transportation
and utilities, labor, education, foreign affairs, and of course,
finance
- Integrated interministerial consultations and coordination at
the highest level of decision making

Public-Private Partnership Concept

To become effective, the private sector is a key if not *the* key player. To
illustrate this point, there were cases in ex-socialist countries in eastern
Europe or central Asia where the state trading corporations had to implement trade promotion abroad in partnership with the public sector. Most
of them had difficulties expanding their business outside their borders
with nontraditional exports. It seemed that it was more difficult for them
to build public-private partnerships, while these are well accepted and
practiced in many open-market economies.

The private sector, therefore, must be fully involved in the overall
process—not just consulted, but involved. The private sector must "buy
in" and feel responsible for the success or failure of the strategy.

The Partnership Process

To initiate the strategy development process, it is necessary to consider
the question of *leadership* and *ownership*:

- Should strategy management be a top-down responsibility (i.e.,
government directed) or a bottom-up exercise (i.e., business led)?
- Should the initiative shift as the strategy moves through the
design, implementation, and evaluation/refinement phases?
What are the institutional implications?

To start the process, it is necessary to define the meaning and
implications of a trade promotion strategy for all the parties, the strategic goals involved, and ways to manage such a strategy. This will be
reviewed in chapter 2.

CHAPTER 2

Defining Trade Promotion and Strategic Goals

Before considering trade promotion programs, it is necessary to define the term and its implications, with the following goals:

- The continuing changes in the international trading environment suggest that trade strategy needs to be reassessed and constantly redefined. This should be done by public-sector strategists.
- The use of the Internet and new technologies for information and communications (NTIC) can drastically improve traditional trade promotion activities like trade missions abroad or participation in professional trade fairs. NTIC may even substitute them with virtual conferences or bids on the Internet through networking, web presence, and so on.
- Similarly, new trade support services are being introduced to increase international competitiveness (e.g., profile market testing online).

This means that new trade promotion programs have to be (re) designed to develop new export capacities, included in the national approach to trade promotion, with all its institutional implications. The method would then be to analyze the need for trade promotion services as a starting point. Such needs assessment, however, may lead to conflicting results. Obviously, needs and priorities may differ, depending on who is being consulted.

Strategic Goals

At that point, some key concerns have to be considered before and during the process of trade promotion–strategy building.

Strategic Goal 1: Awareness Building

From the public-sector perspective, awareness building, development of a national export culture, skills development, and the stimulation of international entrepreneurship are the components of a national export development strategy (NEDS). In reality, it is not very easy to establish a balance between the perceived needs and decide on the proper priorities—for instance, deciding whether to put resources in new markets exploration or in the expansion of existing ones or whether to support newcomers or strengthen existing ones.

Strategic Goal 2: Prioritize Needs Versus Demand

Needs assessment also becomes more complex when the distinction is drawn between actual demand within the business sector for specific trade promotion services and effective need. For instance, it may appear that some services are perceived as most beneficial (e.g., banking services, information on potential buyers, freight forwarding services, potential agents, or distributors) while others are not so essential (e.g., general information on doing business in the country, on trade missions, on export training, or even counseling).

In fact, the export-oriented entrepreneur or manager considers the need for trade promotion services in terms of his or her "demand" for specific types of information and facilitating services. The exporter does not generally perceive the need for trade promotion services in terms of the company's own structural or operational shortcomings—for example, the company may not be able to use commercial intelligence effectively or to correctly manage the export process. Indeed, many exporters are not conscious of their weaknesses in the export business and are not willing to require specific remedial services, even if they are offered.

Consequently, the challenge is how to satisfy the business sector's demand for immediate solutions while concurrently developing higher levels of managerial competency over the long term and the company's capacity to achieve international standards of competitiveness.

A mix of proposed services may be the best option, which could address trade promotion issues in terms of

- development objectives (e.g., gaining a significant market share in the target country),
- meeting existing demand within the business sector for promotion and trade support services,
- building longer-term competitiveness (e.g., increasing comparative cost advantage).

Strategic Goal 3: Targeting the Client

The most critical question for the advisor is, who within the business sector should really be the primary clients? To answer this question a classification can be drawn between a firm's export potential (low, medium, or high) and its support requirement (low, medium, or high).

Client group A would be high export potential with low support requirement

Client group B would be medium and high export potential with medium to high support requirement

Client group C would be low export potential with high support requirement

In the final analysis, the answer will dictate the strategy's overall definition and scope. The obvious response for a group A client is that the strategy should target the exporter with sufficient product/service knowledge and experience—that is, an enterprise with a little promotional support, that can develop existing markets and possibly diversify in new ones. If trade promotion services focus on this target group, the impact of the strategy can be more easily demonstrated within a shorter time.

Another approach could be to concentrate on target groups mostly made up of inexperienced businesses with good export potential but medium to extensive need for support—that is, group B. The risk will be higher, of course, with less obvious impact in the short to medium term. The type of support for group B will be significantly different and certainly more comprehensive than that required by high-potential firms with low export-support requirements. By their mission statements, many trade support institutions will tend to concentrate their efforts on client group B in the absence of strategic direction pressures.

Group B exporters will in all likelihood be more numerous, which means that providing support directly to these firms may strain available resources, both financial and technical. This would suggest that targeting this category may consist of support through industry associations, groups of firms, and clusters, rather than individual companies.

Finally, a third category of potential clients consists of firms with high support requirements and very low export capacity (group C). Logic may suggest that such firms are not a legitimate recipient group, but the tendency has often been for the public sector, in the absence of consultation with business representatives, to rather favor group C clients for strategic reasons of global development capacities. Experience indicates that such initiatives contribute only marginally to export performance and involve a significant opportunity cost, often based on noneconomic considerations.

Strategic Goal 4: Building a Competitiveness Response Capacity

The past 15 years have seen a radical change in the nature of global competition. A trade environment now exists that can be described as hypercompetitive for many products and services. Strategies that focus only on where to export, what to offer, and how to promote products or services are rapidly becoming inadequate.

Today, international trade is characterized by constantly escalating competition among producers and suppliers, rapid product innovation, shorter design and product life cycles, aggressive pricing, and knowledge-based competition. Along with these changes, new approaches have been introduced to serve customer needs with a total competitiveness capacity.

For the majority of traded products, the information and communications revolutions have put the buyer in a stronger bargaining position. The Internet is making more information available to buyers on potential sources of supply. Business-to-Business (B-to-B) e-commerce is now largely implemented even by small and medium-sized enterprises (SMEs) with shorter and shorter product life cycles.

Consequently, exporters who previously competed on the basis of price and quality now are also competing in terms of *response capacity*. Success in the international marketplace is increasingly determined on the basis of the firm's adaptability, flexibility, quick response, communication, and delivery capacity.

In today's global marketplace, exporters, industries, and governments must collectively take the initiative to introduce strategies that will result in a business environment that is truly internationally competitive. According to the former secretary general of the United Nations Council on Trade and Development (UNCTAD), Rubens Recupero, "More and more, the modern economy is knowledge-based and international competitiveness will largely be a function of knowledge. Germany, for example, accounts for 9% of total world coffee export, without growing a single bean." In short, a total competitive response is now required. What are the implications for the national export strategists?

The trade promotion strategy must not only address market identification and market development issues but also facilitate the business sector's adjustment to changing methods of doing business and to the market's rising expectations about the seller's capacity to respond comprehensively and just in time.

This constitutes the new paradigm of business competitiveness.

Strategic Goal 5: Considering National Environment and Clustering to Promote New Capacities

For SMEs in general and developing countries in particular, it is frequent that weaknesses at the production end of the transaction process often represent the greatest constraint to sustained improvement in export performance. These include the following:

- Production inputs that do not meet international specifications
- Technology being inadequate for design or quality requirements and for moving up the value chain
- Insufficient installed capacity for accepting minimum order sizes

At the moment, few export strategies address these domestic issues directly. But planners may have well underestimated the fact that one cannot export products that are not available or cannot be produced. Therefore, defining a trade promotion strategy implies considering domestic product development as a prerequisite.

A strategy that defines trade promotion in the context of export capacity development will involve local programs designed to generate complementarities and synergies within export industries. In this respect, creating capabilities and efficiencies through industrial clusters and networks, reinforcing backward linkages between high performing exporters and local suppliers, and promoting the formation of joint marketing groups have all proven to be relevant approaches for long-term export capacity development and trade promotion.

Export clustering and networking can best be illustrated by the example of EcoHamaca. EcoHamaca is a network of 11 handicraft hammock producers in Masaya, Nicaragua. Each enterprise competes separately on the local market, but they collaborate in developing foreign markets. Designs and production specifications have been standardized in collaboration with wood and furniture producers in the Masaya industrial cluster. Export-oriented production has been consolidated. Pricing has been similarly standardized. The network has acquired legal status and has hired a business development and training manager.

The hammock producers have adopted an ecologically friendly strategy, changing the wood used for poles from a threatened species to more abundant species and using natural instead of chemical dyes. A common label—"Made in Masaya"—has been launched to promote local identity and establish cluster-wide production standards. Eventually, the label will be extended to all handicraft items produced by the cluster.[1]

Strategic Goal 6: Shortening the Steps Toward Internationalization

One strategic approach is to shortcut the export process. Finland, for example, has pushed for the integration of SMEs into the country's export-oriented industrial clusters and has encouraged them to begin international operations from the start, rather than following the traditional route of developing from domestic market to export. But this implies a strong support and in-depth national export-development program.

Canada and, to some extent, Mauritius have also tried to shortcut the internationalization process by supporting the exporter from the very beginning. This will be illustrated further in parts II and III, which are devoted to case studies.

The internationalization process involves several typical steps followed by companies, which then can be classified according to their practices or "know how." These are *the steps toward internationalization*:

Step 1: Accidental interest in exporting. The firm is prepared to fill an unsolicited export order but does not consider the feasibility of exporting through specific adjustment or product/service adaptation (or simply ignores its comparative advantage).

Step 2: Exploring exports opportunities. The firm is actively exploring the feasibility of exporting but is exporting less than 5% of its total sales. Typically the firm undertakes or buys an export market research report for specific target countries.

Step 3: Experimental exporter. The firm is exporting on an experimental basis to not-too-distanced countries (or in a regional agreement area) that are generally close or share a culture similar to that of the domestic market, with export equivalent to more than 5% of total sales.

Step 4: Experienced exporter but in limited scope. Exports go beyond 5% of total sales, and the firm is prepared to adjust its export offers according to the commercial environment but is still exporting to countries that are geographically or culturally close (again in regional, free trade areas).

Step 5: Exporter with confirmed experience. Exports sales are greater than 5% of total sales, and the firm is now considering the expansion to export in additional countries that are distant and have different cultures.[2]

Strategic Goal 7: Lowering the Cost of Doing Business

Reducing the costs of nontrade components—that is, the cost that the enterprise must assume in order to be qualified to export, such as Internet access and quality certification—is also a relevant aspect of a comprehensive national trade development strategy.

Similarly, all programs are designed to reduce the overall export transaction cost, including simplifying procedures and lowering the cost of financial services.

Reducing the Cost of "Non-Tradeables"

ISO 9000 certification is increasingly becoming a prerequisite for firms wishing to export and make progress along the value chain. But the cost of preparing this certification can be too expensive for many firms, especially SMEs.

For example, the trade promotion institution in Mauritius, Enterprise Mauritius, introduced the following scheme:

- Interested enterprises are given guidelines for preparing their proposals for financial support.
- A database on local and international consultants is made available to the enterprises wanting to prepare for ISO 9000 certification.
- Firms are reimbursed half the fees paid for such consultancies, up to a specified ceiling.
- Firms with sufficient in-house expertise to prepare for certification receive up to half the cost (with a ceiling) of sending their quality managers overseas to review the operations of similar firms already having obtained ISO 9000 certification.

The ministry in Mauritius regularly monitors the impact of the plan by assessing participating firms' export performance.

The comparatively high cost of obtaining financing for SMEs from developing countries can be attributed in large part to

- a comparatively high level of risk aversion within the local banking system,
- limited technical capacities for analyzing credit risks,
- the lack of adequate export-related financing schemes.

The national strategy planner can do little to address directly the issue of risk adversity per se—other than, perhaps, to try to convince senior executives in the banking sector to introduce a less risk-adverse culture within their banks. Concerted training to improve the expertise of individual loan officers in analyzing risks and adapting financial solutions to the needs of the export community can partly overcome the financial issue.

Experience indicates that local banks, and particularly those that are not internationally oriented or part of a transnational group, are generally more ready to recognize the need for capacity building through external professional development packages.[3]

More immediate results can be achieved by introducing simplified schemes for the acceptance and discounting of letters of credit (*which typically can reduce the cost for the exporter by more than 50%*).

More complex schemes, such as credit guarantee schemes, which enables banks to off load part of the transaction risk, and price guaranteed contracts for commodities such as coffee or tobacco (as offered by the PTA Bank in Nairobi) would seem to be particularly relevant.

Strategic Goal 8: Reorienting Trade Promotion to Develop Long-Term Relationships

Studies confirm that the cost of finding a new customer is three times more than the cost of maintaining an existing customer. This suggests that a national trade promotion program should be reoriented toward systematic market development and promotion efforts. This means going away from helping exporters to look for spot-contract basis—which is the tendency of many trade support programs—and toward assisting the local business community in developing long-term supply relationships.

This means targeting multinational companies that are outsourcing a growing part of their production or service requirements. Of course, in international business, competition is fierce and comparative advantages are constantly challenged by newcomers, but this point should not be overestimated. Multinational corporations appreciate established relationships and do not shift their business to unknown newcomers unless they have strong reasons to do so.

Could Trade Promotion Be Directed to Foreign Direct Investment (FDI)?

Reorienting trade promotion activities to pursue long-term commercial relationships and develop new export capacity raises the issue of whether the strategy should encompass investment promotion. This issue has led to different solutions, with some countries preferring to develop FDI in different institutions other than trade promotion organizations (TPOs), on the basis that investment is more a matter of finance than pure trade promotion activities, involving more marketing and market access issues than finance.

However, for many developing countries, attracting FDI is the most rational way to acquire new export capacity of an international competitive standard, obtain immediate market access, and generate dynamic competitive advantages. As a result, the promotion of FDI has become a major feature of national trade promotion strategies in Asia (e.g., China, India, and the Association of Southeast Asian Nations [ASEAN] "tigers").

Conclusion

Taking these eight goals into account will require trade-promotion planners to redefine the traditional approach to trade promotion. And the larger the number of challenges they decide to incorporate into trade promotion, the greater the number and diversity of functions and organizations that will need to be engaged in the strategy development and management process.

This will be reviewed in the next two chapters, which will discuss process building and strategic linkages, respectively.

CHAPTER 3

Setting Up the Process of Trade Promotion Strategy

Export Development and Export Promotion

As the performance of several countries with high export performance confirms, effective strategies are based on a continuous process involving design, implementation, monitoring and evaluation, feedback, and refinement. Yet national strategy planners must be involved in all phases of the strategic cycle. Indeed, all members of the national strategy management team—both public and private—must participate in one way or another throughout the cycle.

One of the lessons learned by successful exporting countries is that while the public sector is the catalyst in the strategy development and management process, to be effective, the strategy must be "owned" by the private sector.

Strategy design is therefore most effective when its development and refinement comes from the bottom up, with industry representatives and managers working directly with public-sector officials to establish priorities.

Partnership can be viewed as an ongoing synchronized process through strategic spirals, run in parallel by the public and private sector with different roles:

1. Planning and design
   - Public sector: Needs analysis, priority setting, and dialogue initiation
   - Private sector: Sectoral priority setting/exporter consensus

2. Coordination and implementation
   - Public sector: Facilitation and support
   - Private sector: Implementation
3. Monitoring and evaluation
   - Public sector: Methodology/analysis
   - Private sector: Information gathering and reporting
4. Feedback and Refinement
   - Public sector: Strategy adjustment/public information
   - Private sector: Advice/direction

Foreign Trade Policies Are Expressed at the National Level

The announcement of a foreign trade policy at the national level helps set priorities and enables business executives to count on clear support over at least the medium term. This, therefore, helps build and implement export business plans that have stronger impacts on foreign markets.

Resistance to Open National Trade Policies

Many executives who do not see government intervention as a valuable assistance in principle would support such policies only when they are faced with direct competition against competing businesses who benefit from strong government support (claiming unfair competing practices).

In fact, even those who are against public support do not reject direct or indirect assistance when they need reliable information or help for logistics or information, among other services. Many opponents to such support policies think that most of the time assistance is inefficient and fails to make the best use of existing resources. However, opponents to such policies often accept assistance from trade commissioners to acquire official information on the creditworthiness of foreign operators or from, say, the official export credit support for an export credit guarantee bank. Beyond this, some business executives in fact neglect or avoid public assistance, claiming that in return of support, confidentiality is threatened and competition may use their trade contacts. This is a typical behavior within joint export marketing groups created or promoted under public assistance and operating on common stands within professional trade fairs.

Export Development and Export Promotion Involve Complementary Policies

With the growing liberalization of world trade, within the rules set up by the World Trade Organization (WTO), there is a fierce competition for gaining increased market shares with open support of governments (e.g., in the agricultural or services sectors). This means state support actions are part of the tools used for facilitating trade, sometimes even designed by the business sector with government support. Both the private and public sector are involved in trade support policies At this point, a distinction should be made between *export promotion* and *export development.*

Export development aims at producing new export products or services and/or penetrating new markets that were not accessible before. Therefore, the aim of export development consists of identifying existing opportunities or technologies and expanding new industries and production facilities to meet—sometimes to generate—new demands on the market.

So, to a great extent, export development concentrates on product and service adaptation, reengineering (and sometimes creating new) production processes or supply chains to access new markets that are more profitable than traditional outlets. The export development approach clearly requires more effort, resources, and persistence than the simple traditional export promotion approach. It means that trade policies implemented at business or state level may engage more resources in export development than in export promotion.

Also, a lack of resources (or technological capacity) may induce limits that force exporters to limit themselves to export promotion actions only. However, this does not mean that export promotion and export development are distinct activities. They are complementary, with proper balance between them, based on the relative capacity of the agents to invest more on one side (export promotion focusing on trade facilitation and market access) than on the other (export development focusing on investing in new outlets and creating new markets).

Most economies now recognize that export promotion and trade development are a "national priority" to achieve economic and social goals. Governments expect that sustained efforts will help to earn foreign (hard) currency, reducing indebtedness, balance payment disequilibrium, create additional employment, and so on.

Export development is not only desirable but indispensable for countries that have a narrow export base in terms of product range. This is not merely limited to developing countries with single or few export commodity resources (e.g., the Ivory Coast with cocoa). In such cases, export promotion efforts cannot be put on commodity-based products, since the amount of promotional expenses has no influence on the sale of goods whose price is dictated exclusively by the balance between offer and demand on a single mechanical scale (moreover within an uncontrollable volatility range). This is also true for some commodity-rich countries, which may have the temptation to rely only on one sector for foreign exchange and will see their dependency increased (which is the case of Ghana). Conscious of that danger, some countries have realized that they have to make heavy investments in expanding their export base through export development programs, like the *Emirates* (Dubai, Qatar) who are promoting services—airlines, cultural and educational services, business tourism, and so on. One can note that promotional campaigns from these countries are clearly national. For these oil-rich Middle Eastern countries, export promotion and trade development in "noncommodity" products have become a national priority.

In many environments, it is frequently thought that carrying out export development and export promotion programs implies substantive resources that are scarce, limited, or simply unavailable within companies or in local trade support institutions like chambers of commerce and industry associations. This not only applies in developing countries but also in some sectors or regions of developed economies. Such resources (mainly financial, through export credit loans, for instance, or trade information on foreign markets) have to be provided by government agencies. The development strategy of a country will set the stage for fixing the level and type of trade linkages with international markets, as illustrated by the example of Taiwan, province of China.

A Short History of Economic Development of Taiwan, Province of China: Spreading the Export Range

In the late 1940s, Taiwan, province of China, had been a predominately agrarian economy based on rice and sugar production. Agricultural output was then taking off, following land reforms set up by the government. The agricultural surplus, as well as the aid from the United States in the early 1950s, helped to concentrate attention on developing the industrial base. These efforts were successful for industrial output, which rose by 240% from 1952 to 1960.

In the 1960s, transnational corporations (TNCs), mainly from the United States, became established in Taiwan. But under the Taiwanese government's foreign investment control, only TNCs that could provide a high rate of technology transfer were accepted.

However, when the small size of the domestic market and the end to U.S. foreign aid threatened this early success, special programs were launched that aimed at promoting export-oriented industries, which sparked spectacular growth for Taiwan in the 1960s and 1970s.

By the 1980s, wages were rising sharply, with a direct impact on the cost of mass production of low-value consumer goods, which was becoming too expensive to compete in world markets. This led Taiwan to encourage the development of capital- and technology-intensive industries like electronics and chemicals.

One major feature of economic growth was the presence of well-developed and enterprising SMEs, many of which were in the export business. The government believed that larger firms could exploit economies of scale and therefore set up support structures to help SMEs form strategic alliances with foreign firms.

At present, lower-value manufactures have shifted overseas to lower-cost locations. This has reduced the share of manufacturing in gross domestic product (GDP). Furthermore, the Taiwanese government strongly promoted growth in the services sector, which increased its share, which is expected to approach 70% in 2015.

Therefore, the pattern of exports has also been dramatically changing, as exports to traditional developed markets like the United States have expanded globally and exports to developing economies have increased. (The Taiwan market share of textile and electronic products in Africa has taken a dominant position.) Taiwan remains one of the most dynamic exporting countries in the world.[1]

Policy Formulation and Implementation of Export Promotion Measures

Government trade promotion policy decision on export development strategies, established in term of appropriate instruments to use for developing promotional measures, is critical for national foreign trade performance.[2]

According to a World Bank report, countries with efficient trade promotion policies appear to grow faster than others, the underlying support factor being that at the global level, exports have grown faster than GDP. Over the last 3 decades (1980–2010), global GDP has been growing 2.7% a year, while global trade grew 5.7% a year. Over the last 2 decades, these figures were 2.3 and 6.5%, respectively.[3]

Export Development as a Strategic Choice

All countries, whether they are developed, in development, or emerging economies, are considering export development as a major tool for growth, either for expanding their market shares in foreign markets or for acquiring access in new markets alone or through joint partnership. Such goals are strategic in the way that they imply long-term commitment and sustained efforts to reach their objectives and require structural adjustments at the national level for getting the required competitiveness to "make the difference."

For many countries, especially in developing and emerging economies, export-oriented production tends to be more labor intensive than production oriented for the domestic market, therefore creating employment. These (successful) export-oriented strategic development policies are best illustrated by Singapore, Hong Kong, Mauritius, Sri Lanka, or by medium-sized developed countries like Finland and New Zealand. Such policies imply setting strong trade promotion strategies.

Export Trade Has Its Own Exigencies

Exporting is highly competitive and constantly changing. Price competition is intensive because foreign buyers increasingly rely on outsourcing and business-to-business production processes, with shorter product life cycles pushing for timely delivery. Only producers and countries that can keep up with these pressures will benefit from increased globalization. So the challenge is to ensure that trade promotion policies translate the identified need to thrust foreign trade priorities into profit opportunities.

With the effective globalization of trade, the promotion of exports is universally viewed by governments around the world as a public function, which is universally recognized as generating jobs, providing strong incentive to productivity increases, and projecting the nation's brand image into global markets.

Comparative Advantages for New National Trade Promotion Networks

Today, however, diplomacy has acquired a commercial focus in many countries, with most goals defined in economic, not political, terms. For this reason, countries that never built a global diplomacy network have the advantage of focus.

The case of Mexico is a good example: Mexico's Bancomext (now Pro-México) operates in only 22 countries, with multiple offices in the largest markets. France, by comparison, maintains embassies in 166 countries with significant commercial activity in most of them. Not surprisingly, Mexico spends less than a third of what France spends on export promotion (as a percentage of its exports).

Are National Trade Promotion Programs Responsible for Trade Growth?

A more in-depth analysis, however, reveals that many national export promotion program expenditures are considered more wasteful than cost-effective. Such feelings are mostly expressed by large companies rather than medium-sized ones.

To that extent, it could be noted that most of the export gains realized over the last decades in the world markets were induced by the systematic expansion of supply chain trade links generated by multinational corporations abroad, the lowering of trade tariffs, and the improved efficiency of international communications, helping to link customers and manufacturers around the world with no reference to explicit national trade promotion programs.

That being said, some large countries do take a return-on-investment approach to ensure the effective use of their trade promotion budgets and encourage their exporters to develop highly effective programs at the regional or sectoral level.

CHAPTER 4

Competitiveness Issues Are Defined at the National Level

The Growing Role of National Initiatives to Promote Trade

It is essential to consider that with increased global competition, governments have become increasingly important for companies' success, as they need to benefit from the best possible environment at the national level. Companies are under pressure, with strong competitive home-based suppliers, ever-more demanding local customers, and growing foreign (importing) market requirements that force them to innovate constantly. They have to deploy their resources in a forward-looking, dynamic, and challenging national environment within the established and predictable rules of national culture and economic structures, where supporting institutions (local and national) play a dominant role.[1]

This national favorable environment can make the difference in competitiveness. Nations succeed in particular industries or services because their home environment is the most forward looking, at infrastructural and institutional levels. A clear illustration is given by Singapore, which has a strong support policy for its enterprises.

In such a context, business executives are pressing for more government support for particular industries, not only for protective schemes but also for supporting measures like trade agreements, favorable investment borrowing conditions, and export credit guarantee schemes. It has been fully recognized, for instance, that competitiveness—through the Davos Group productivity index ranking—is directly linked to strong national support environments (e.g., the case of Switzerland).

Definitely, this approach to the nation's role in export development and trade is applying the concept of Michael Porter: "National Competitiveness has become one of the central preoccupations of government and industry in every nation."

Despite the statement made by Michael Porter that the notion of a competitive nation is not well defined while the notion of a company is well established,[2] the role played by international organizations, even by international conferences like the G20 meetings, is definitely growing. These institutions are setting rules and norms in trade. Nations are players who are directly negotiating, which illustrates their still-growing influence on the global arena. As can be seen, a competitive-nation role is clearly visible, by forming alliances or creating pressure groups which then govern world trade agreements.

Ultimately, the absence of competitive capacity understood and supported by nations may result in resistance to change, which unfortunately drives to threats and delays in agreeing. This is illustrated by the Doha Round's hard-to-reach agreements after 10 years of unsuccessful negotiations.

New theories recognize that in international competition, companies compete with global strategies merging trade and foreign investment (value of currency and investment in US dollars or in euros, as illustrated by the Chinese foreign trade policy): "A new theory must move beyond comparative advantage of a nation. It must reflect a rich conception of competition that includes segmented markets, differentiated products, technology differences, and economies of scale."[3]

This underlines the key role of home-based institutions and regulatory environments. This also explains why there is a sort of competition of comparative advantages offered by host countries to attract investments and to allow for better treatment of companies established in a given location. This may drive to favor "competitive currency devaluation," denounced in 2011 by the G20 as a "bad practice." Artificial devaluation slippage does not allow for better competitiveness, even if it is perceived as beneficial in the short term. It has an impact as long as the other partners do not adjust their own currency or leave the monetary market to do so.

The Patterns of Success in International Markets and Trade Promotion

The main success factors for companies that have achieved international leadership are linked with their trade promotion strategies.[4] All companies showing international leadership may have employed trade promotion strategies that differ from each other, but their underlying mode of operation follows similar patterns.

They all have competitive advantages through developing and implementing innovation processes over their foreign markets. De facto, home markets are not necessarily different from foreign markets from the company's product and service-range point of view; just their strength and weaknesses analysis, which can be different from one market to another, with the corresponding applied marketing strategies.

Innovation process is seen in the broadest sense, meaning the application of new technologies and/or new processes that could be translated as a new vision of manufacturing a product or providing a service. This can be achieved by a reengineering process (new product/service) but also by applying a better combination of production factors, whether such factors are available at home or in global markets, where the competition is also active for providing the best possible combination in cost/quality.

The broad meaning of new processes may also mean a better marketing approach, new investments in skills and knowledge access, as well as brand image. That means small incremental steps over time may achieve the same results as a major breakthrough in a short period.

In international markets, innovation can generate competitive advantages by serving entirely new market segments that competition has neglected or opening new avenues on different foreign markets that are not at the same development level (e.g., serving the Chinese market segments in east coast cities with high-tech or fashion products and services for eager consumers whose purchasing power is increasing rapidly). When competitors are slow to respond, the competitiveness means the ability to quickly offer the product and service at accepted market prices. For example, Toyota has gained a global competitiveness advantage in offering hybrid cars at least 2 years before other car manufacturers could offer similar vehicles, contributing to its number one world position as a car manufacturer while General Motors was near bankruptcy. There were attempts to reduce Toyota's success by questioning their brakes and speed control, but even a justified recall did not hamper their success.

Similarly, the environment and concern for sustainable development create huge opportunities for companies that are ready to deploy new energy-saving processes. The real concern is to provide sufficient financial support to such innovative industries.

What would be the best practice for a trade promotion organization (TPO) in such context? Obviously, it would be to inform investors that they can benefit from favorable financing conditions for investing, moreover providing some kind of export-credit guarantee for the banks facilitating access to foreign markets.

Timely and relevant information plays a key role in implementing innovation processes, but there is certain information that is not available to competitors or that they do not seek. At that point, TPOs play a major role in providing market research findings. Desk or field research on foreign markets is time consuming and expensive, particularly for medium-sized companies. Field research can be implemented by the national network of trade commissioners or trade representatives, who may conduct such research at a cost if local resources are limited.

Sometimes innovators come from another sector or industry or some foreign contact, seeing opportunities with a clear vision, or may even come from inside the company itself, but their point of view is often ignored or set aside. In the 1990s, systematic inside company policies were initiated by Japanese transnational corporations (TNCs) to award staff providing any constructive ideas on the manufacturing process, even at the lowest level of responsibility, and such initiatives have since been reproduced in other companies.

To advise individual companies, export promotion organizations may first need to obtain recognition and acceptance for their innovative ideas. For example, the French Foreign Trade Centre (Le Centre Français du Commerce Extérieur [CFCE]) undertook a study of the world market for machine tools which concluded that only numerically controlled machine tools could be competitive on the world market. However, some leading manufacturers stated that such product development would need further research and development. The French Foreign Trade Centre agreed to finance the process to overcome their apprehension.

However, innovation usually occurs within competing environments. Almost any advantage can be quickly copied: South Korea imitated

Japanese LED television screens to achieve improvements that surpassed Japanese competitors (Samsung over Sony) at lower costs. Brazil produced commercial aircrafts for civil aviation based on European models and can now successfully compete with Europe, particularly in developing countries.

It is clear that TPOs, through their networks of trade representatives, may indicate to their companies where to find technology and how to acquire it—including through partnerships. Such a policy of gathering information and finding partners has been systematically applied in China over decades of export/import partnerships, which was even a precondition for selling to the Chinese market (e.g., the Volkswagen and Fiat compete to penetrate the market). In this area, the role of TPOs is sometimes essential because it brings credibility during the information gathering phase (and even during the negotiation phase), when the home company has access to limited information.

Companies that stop innovating are promptly challenged by competition. Sometimes early-mover advantages, such as loyal customers, benefits from economies of scale, or strong franchising policies, can help to retain market dominance for a limited time only. Sooner or later, more dynamic rivals take the opportunity and find a better or less-expensive way to manufacture or provide the same product or service.

It is well known that Chinese providers for electrical appliances have replaced the traditional Italian or even German suppliers in the large retail chains. The only response for Italian and German suppliers would have been to develop strong brand franchises, which was undertaken by German manufacturers.

In such areas, the TPO sometimes may have difficulties warning the foreign (home-based) supplier that the local price conditions are changing and that suppliers' prices are rising. This monitoring service is difficult to implement, even if the Internet may help, because local information is not easily available, nor is it easy to gather. In such cases, a special link should be established in the supply chain, for instance through the trade commissioner (or through any other business organization like the manufacturer's association or the chamber of commerce). In fact, confidentiality of supply conditions is the only limit beyond which information is restricted throughout the concerned partners' network.

The best approach to retain a competitive advantage is to upgrade the product or service. This process is well known in the software industry. Moving to more services, through online subscription (preferably automated) discourages the user from finding other products, with a corresponding high learning curve, for both the individual user and the trained staff. This process is perfectly illustrated by Microsoft, innovating software in newer Windows or Office versions thus making the transition to other alternative software difficult. Competitors in open-source software, while free of charge, still have a difficult gap to overcome to take a significant market share.

In this large software industry, one predominant feature is a systematic global strategy approach, with appropriate communication. However, in this field, transnational corporations (TNC) are the only players and the TPOs are being marginalized. From product design to market penetration and marketing, the whole business is handled by the TNC itself, whether it is Apple, Microsoft, Sun-Oracle, or any other supplier. Moreover, it is such a global issue that national identity is no longer perceived (focusing instead on the founder's name only), but the constant update has been well implemented.

As this case shows, innovation and change are closely linked. But change is not natural or easily carried out. It is well known that large TNCs have difficulties questioning their own processes, since they are institutionalized in a "vertical" process (top-down) that cannot be easily overthrown, particularly in successful companies.

In TNCs, inside training and strong established procedures are well stated. In such a business environment, there is only one correct way to do business, as the existing strategy is firmly established by the hierarchy and implemented. To question it is to face the whole credibility of the TNC and its decision-making process. This drives some rigidity—or at least some lack of flexibility—that does not help in making quick adjustments when challenges occur.

Limited flexibility of TNCs does not encourage them to seek advice and assistance from TPOs, which explains why TNCs are traditionally not their clients. However, sometimes the TNCs approach TPOs to assess their own market findings. But unfortunately too often they do not share their own conclusions, including with small companies who are not a threat to their position.

CHAPTER 5

The Competitiveness Scheme in the Context of Trade Promotion Strategies

Institutional Linkages

At national level, the type of institutional linkages and functional relationships should first be reviewed in order to ensure that a broad-based strategy is formulated, implemented, and reflected through the various action plans initiated by the organizations directly involved in the export development effort. It is essential that all stakeholders participate in the process and secure political commitments for successful implementation of the strategy.

Adopting the Principles at National Level

The goal is to build national consensus and commitment and to maintain functioning partnerships at all concerned levels within the public sector, between the public and private sector, among trade institutions, and within the business community. These consensus, however, could not be so easy to reach, since, in general, the public and private sector representatives have no established structure for exchanging their views on trade promotion strategies It may happen, however, that such an exercise creates new links through the communication channels established for this purpose (e.g., through an ad hoc national commission).

Implications for the National Trade Promotion Organization

Once the principle of developing a plan for national trade promotion has been adopted, a fully integrated national export development strategy has to be set up. At that stage, national trade promotion organizations (TPO) are involved; as key actors in this process, they have to be proactive since they contribute to the export strategy building process. In some countries, unfortunately, TPOs do not have the proper status or mandate to do so. Moreover, most national trade promotion organizations have limited resources (both in personnel and in budget allocation) to take the lead role. The TPO involved could then negotiate with the national trade policy authorities to have adequate resources for playing their role and for implementing proper action plans (it may happen that the TPO acts on behalf of the national authorities).

Assessing the Process

Such process, defined as a national export development strategy (NEDS) must be perceived by all actors as being effective and implemented by the concerned authorities, with proper public budgets and expenditures. Therefore, assessment of benefits and impact should be included in the process to refine and adjust both the strategy itself and the implementation process.

Building an Ongoing Process

In setting up the process, "competitiveness drivers" measurement should be included and considered as part of the building This has various implications for the development of key components that play a role in competitiveness, like e-commerce facilities, the impact of multinationals, the growing trend of global outsourcing, to name some.

More specifically, such types of questions should be addressed (this is not an exhaustive list):

- What is the role of the public sector in assisting local firms to find their way along the Internet and e-business?
- What steps must be taken to ensure that local companies can be part of international outsourcing programs of multinationals and other foreign companies?
- What should be the priorities of the public-sector strategy builder?

Answering these questions helps to assist the NEDS's building process, in order to develop a response to the challenges of today's competitive marketplace. Obviously, here there are more questions than answers. But this building process provides an incentive among stakeholders for creating or strengthening partnerships all over the global environment. Of course, such a process involves a continuous dialogue between trade promotion officials and the business community.

Building a National Competitiveness Framework

To illustrate the above process, a good example is given by a survey made in 2005 by the *Commonwealth Secretariat* providing a list of requirements for developing a proper environment for national competitiveness:

- A stable, predictable macroeconomic environment for enterprise development, characterized by low budget deficits, tight inflation control and competitive real exchange rates
- An outward-oriented market-friendly trade and industrial regime emphasizing the dismantling of import controls and tariffs
- A proactive foreign investment strategy which
  o targets a few realistic sectors and host countries,
  o views overseas promotional offices as public-private partnerships,
  o provides competitive investment incentives,
  o streamlines investment-approval processes
- Sustained development in human capital at all levels (particularly tertiary, scientific, information technology and engineering education) and increased enterprise training (including assistance for industry associations to launch training schemes, information campaigns to educate firms about the benefit of training and tax breaks for training)
- Comprehensive technology support for quality management, productivity improvement, metrology and technical support services for small and medium-sized enterprises (SMEs) (including grants to obtain ISO 9000 certification),

the creation of productivity centers, and commercialization of public technology institutions

- Access to ample industrial finance at competitive interest rates
- An efficient and cost-competitive infrastructure in air and sea cargo, telecommunications, Internet access and power resources[1]

In fact, most of these measures and policies have their results recorded through Enabling Trade Index (ETI),[2] which is published by the World Economic Forum (WEF) every year. The WEF ranking can be considered as a good benchmarking tool for measuring the efficiency of trade promotion strategies.

The ETI measures the extent to which individual economies have developed institutions, policies, and services facilitating the free flow of goods over borders and to destination.

The structure of the Index reflects the main enablers of trade, breaking them into four overall issue areas, captured in the subindexes:

1. The *market access subindex* measures the extent to which the policy framework of the country welcomes foreign goods into the economy and enables access to foreign markets for its exporters.

2. The *border administration subindex* assesses the extent to which the administration at the border facilitates the entry and exit of goods.

3. The *transport and communications infrastructure subindex* takes into account whether the country has in place the transport and communications infrastructure necessary to facilitate the movement.[3]

The trade agreements and trade preferences have been integrated in the 2010 ETI. Results for the 10 best enabling countries are as follows: Singapore, Hong Kong, Denmark, Sweden, Switzerland, New Zealand, Norway, Canada, Luxembourg, and the Netherlands.[4]

New Factors of Competitiveness on the Global Place

The evolution on the international marketplace is continuously driven by a number of forces that affect the way business is conducted. These forces are playing in a favorable or unfavorable environment reflected in the above described ETI, and can be named as competitiveness factors. Such factors changed the way business is conducted, creating new opportunities, closing others. In fact, these factors influence the decision and action taken at the level of individual enterprise both locally and internationally and may involve a fundamental redefinition of the way companies organize and conduct their business.

While the decision to move or not in foreign markets rests entirely with the enterprise's management, the *public sector is definitely in charge of the facilitator's role*. The public sector's responsibility is to ensure that the appropriate business environment is in place to support a suitable response by the private sector. This is the essential component to a successful partnership when the implementation phase is developed. It is generally accepted to consider the following issues and requirements as key for success: rapid response required, participation in global supply chain and capability to offer products' services as a single package.

Altogether, these factors constitute a new definition of the *global response capability* that will shape the environment at the levels of enterprise, enterprise networks, and even in the supply chain.

Competitiveness Factor 1: Capacity to Respond Quickly and Efficiently

Many product life cycles are shortening as a result of innovation and rapid expansion of new manufactured products for industrial or consumer goods. Is is frequent to observe a typical competitive advantage that is ten times shorter than it was ten years ago. This is due to higher levels of competition in the international marketplace, increasingly putting pressure to reduce working capital tied up in production—with subcontracts given abroad to production centers using lower-cost capital, new supply pipelines, and reduced inventories (just-in-time process). Pressure on order sizes is forcing importing companies to demand tighter order-to-delivery response time.

The global fashion clothing industry, for example, used to produce four models a year, and is now forced to work on producing seven or eight models every year (if willing to remain considered on the business-to-business market place), forcing the cycle time from design to shop delivery to fall under 2 months.

Now more than ever flexibility and capacity to respond quickly is a decisive factor for the supplier. Applying modern technologies and extensively using information networks and facilities are the tools used by competing companies to introduce new efficiencies, particularly in search of reduced sourcing times, to improve their supply chain. Such companies now expect their suppliers, both local and foreign, to introduce similar processes and equivalent levels of efficiency.

The immediate effect has been to increase competition among suppliers.

To respond effectively to this increasing emphasis on rapid response, the enterprise manager must do the following:

- Introduce more efficiency into the supply chain (eventually consider new supply channels) and establish suitable contingency plans to overcome long-term bottlenecks and potential production disruption, this assessed on a permanent and continuous basis
- Acquire the necessary quality certification required by the markets the company wishes to enter, even if this is a costly process
- Introduce innovation on technology and processes to provide accurate products and services and deliver systematic information to buyers while maintaining regular and immediate communication with all parties in the buyer's supply chain
- Build a total communication system with current and prospective buyers on a regular/frequent basis

While the required improvements or initiative in these fields obviously rests within and inside the enterprise, the role of the public sector is directly linked, to ensure that the export strategy efforts are supported with rapid response, specifically, by doing the following:

- Reinforcing linkages to local suppliers of production inputs
- Streamlining export procedures and requirements

- Promoting the development of quality certification services
- Establishing national facilities for business-to-business electronic commerce and reducing communication costs (e.g., promoting voice over IP communication)
- Improving transport competitiveness and infrastructure facilities

An Innovative Approach to Rapid Response: The Case of Ukraine and E-Commerce Local Centers

Despite its limited telecommunication infrastructure, Ukraine has, as part of its national export strategy, pushed enterprises to introduce the idea of rapid response to meet new market requirements.

Based on the traditional cooperatives of the Soviet regime, e-commerce centers have been established in specific industrial and agricultural centers outside Kiev where telecoms and information technology limitations hamper local enterprises from having access to the Internet. These e-commerce centers act as electronic post boxes for the local export community, connected via dedicated modems and servers to Kiev where the infrastructure is fairly good. These e-commerce centers not only receive and send e-mails on behalf of local businesses but also propose e-commerce promotional services like development of web sites and pages for these enterprises, thus supporting their overall promotional effort.

Competitiveness Factor 2: Capacity to Be in the Global Supply Chain

In many developed countries (and gradually even for large companies in emerging economies) manufacturers are seeking to maximize efficiencies and to remain competitive, as multinational corporations have been doing for so long. They are restructuring their supply chain by outsourcing major elements of their businesses, in production, logistics, customer service, and administration.

To that extent, the concept of *virtual company* is becoming a reality. This means that a company limits itself to its defined core operations and to the marketing and management of its brand, and outsources all other non-core business activities. This rising trend presents major economical opportunities (maximizing the production factors where they are

the most beneficial). However, the success of local enterprises in secur-
ing foreign outsourcing operations will also depend to a large extent, at
national and institutional level, on the efficiency of import procedures
and banking processes—all of which must be addressed through a supporting infrastructure developed as a consistent national export strategy.

Global sourcing has become a mainstream strategy of transnational corporations, both large and small. However, approaches differ
significantly among transnationals, even among product lines within
companies (depending on the type of business involved). *Many base
their sourcing decisions primarily on cost-reduction considerations (sometimes regulatory and fiscal advantages offered by host countries).* However,
such trends have some common characteristics; they usually limit their
involvement to short-term contractual relationships, constantly analyzing
the comparative advantage of one country's production location against
other possibilities. This becomes a business on its own, known as *efficiency seeking.*

One case goes against such expanding practices, applying a more
sophisticated business ethic: IKEA signs a 3-year supply agreement
with subcontract companies (most of them in developing countries or
countries in transition) on the basis of a very thorough description of
services required, a supply calendar, agreed prices, and a thorough quality control provided by headquarters. But this kind of *mutual chart* is
rather the exception.

On the national side, it is frequent to find offers and incentives by some
developing countries that consider themselves more competitive (e.g., on
cost of labor) than other offers (e.g., Vietnam versus China's east coast).

Effectiveness-seeking transnationals, on the other hand, are more concerned with achieving quality, reliability, and rapid product-development
cycles and are more likely to undertake direct investment, promote skills
transfer, and integrate suppliers into their product design and development
processes (notably when local customization is involved). Obviously, there
are advantages for exporting enterprises to seek partnerships with these two
types of transnationals (as well with the IKEA type of partnership agreement). Naturally, a different type of promotional approach is required for
each—a fact that should be reflected not only in the export strategy of the
export supplier but also in the national export strategy.

Support Without Control: South Asian Cases

Some programs are sponsored by the public sector that link SMEs to larger firms as subcontractors. These programs have been introduced in China, the Republic of Korea, and Singapore.

The most successful ones help to coordinate the output of a number of smaller suppliers to make them more attractive to large firms as exporters. Part of the secret of their success is that the TPO in each of these countries has provided strong support without assuming tight control.

Competitiveness Factor 3: Capacity to Offer Total Product's Service Package

Increasing use of the Internet by sellers has given multinational companies easy access to information on prices, availability of products, and product innovations. This is making the *service package* a key component in the value added chain.

Exporters who concentrate purely on product delivery are likely to lose out to product suppliers who can add an associated package of transactional and post-transactional services. A good example is given in the following case about UK/Vietnam bicycle production.

Table 5.1. A Comparison of the Global Sourcing Strategies of Efficiency-Seeking and Effectiveness-Seeking Multinationals

Global sourcing	Efficiency-seeking	Effectiveness-seeking
Management needs	Capable purchasing managers	Transfer to a sufficient number of engineers and other technical staff
Short-term consequences	Lower cost and improved profitability	Some cost reduction
Intermediate-term consequences	Reduced design and engineering capabilities at home	Integration of research and development engineering and production skills
Long-term consequences	Dependence on independent overseas suppliers that could become potential competitors	Transfer of technology to local network of second-tier suppliers

Source: Adapted from Masaaki (1998).

Value Adding Through a Service Package in Vietnam

Under an initial sourcing arrangement, a bicycle assembler in the United Kingdom imported bicycle components like pedals, cranks, and cotter pins from Vietnam—10 to a box. The boxes were labeled with the bicycle assembler's address and the producer's part number. Separate groups of SMEs from one region in Vietnam produced each part.

The assembly facility in the UK employed three people in its reception warehouse to unpack, clean, grease, label, and repack the correct parts together before they were taken out to the assembly line.

Now the Vietnamese producer assembles and greases the parts before packing for shipment in single units labeled with the bicycle model number. The units are delivered straight to the assembly line in the UK facility.

The delivered price for each part is slightly higher than before, but the assembler saves more than the extra cost in reduced handling, and assembly line disruptions owing to part mix-ups are minimized, thereby adding value.

The Public Sector's Role on Business Competitiveness and Environment

The lesson drawn from all the above mentioned statements is that international competitiveness does not go by itself on the business place. For instance, in countries where highly protective practices or tariffs have been maintained, multinational manufacturing investors complain that they have difficulties in finding local suppliers who can meet their requirements. In the same way, potential commercial partners may avoid making long-term commitments when they consider they would conduct their operations in an inadequate local business environment. Such inadequacies can range from poor physical and social infrastructures to contradictory policies, from nonavailability of competitive local suppliers to a conservative bureaucracy.

The Wrong Way to Make It

In making exhaustive efforts to attract foreign direct investments, one developing country, after long negotiations with a large foreign transnational, made strong commitments to improve its regulatory framework in order to get a manufacturing plant installed in the country.

In the first instance, the foreign company was quite pleased to discover sourcing opportunities for much of its primary and secondary materials directly in the host country. However, it quickly appeared that the national supply chain remained inefficient. There was an imbalance between local tariffs and agreed FDI preferential incentives, together with difficult local communication and administrative infrastructure. Despite efforts (and time) to overcome these obstacles, within 3 years the manufacturing plant had no other choice than importing 95% of its requirements. It became also obvious that the low level of local employee know-how and education kept productivity standards below expectation and wages were forced down to retain some profitability.

From experience, it appears that fiscal incentives should not be used to offset negative aspects of trade environment (legal, regulatory, or infrastructure). These obstacles need to addressed first, if not solved. Fiscal compensation is not the way to waive the obstacles.

Foreign Investment Attraction Policy
Should Include Proper Facilities

A good example is given by Mumbai, India, recognized as providing very efficient new port facilities. Mumbai has therefore recorded a large increase in multinational companies willing to establish their production facilities, to such an extent that there is a competition between foreign companies wishing to be installed there. Mumbai Port authorities are recognized for the quality of services offered, availability of qualified manpower, as well as efficient infrastructures.

Definitely, tax incentives, business opportunities offered, or marketing efforts do not compensate an unattractive bureaucracy and an unpredictable or unreliable supply environment. This is an era in which the public-sector agents can make a direct influence.

For foreign investors as well as for local exporters, the same concern is raised with intellectual property right issues. If these are not addressed, innovative ideas, operational expertise, and transfer of technologies can severely be limited, the operators can just refrain from investment, and government efforts or incentive offered can just have no effects.

Public Procurement Is Somewhat Neglected

There is also a domain that is frequently set aside by exporters, the *public procurement sector*. Until now, many exporters in developing or transition economies do not participate in the public procurement activities of developed markets, estimated to account for up to 20% of their gross domestic product. The World Trade Organization (WTO) Government Procurement Agreement is still the subject of (heavy) discussions for streamlining its provisions and according special and differential treatment to exporters coming from developing countries. This global opportunity is not yet considered, particularly in the service sector, where the Doha Round tries to liberalize market access.

The same remarks apply for the European Union, where member countries grant at least equal treatment for service-sector foreign providers' bid offers. Public-sector strategy makers should keep these developments in mind when formulating their export promotion and development programs.

Conclusion

Competitiveness factors operate in private as well as in public sectors. The competitiveness factors managed by the export business do not operate in isolation, but in a given environment. Exporting companies are acting in places where the public sector play a key role in developing and managing the best possible business conditions. These competitiveness factors are also in action among nations when they are candidates for hosting FDI and other transnational partners. This is what strategic planners should have in mind when export development programs are planned and managed.

CHAPTER 6

Key Components for Successful Promotion Activities

The most successful trade promotion organizations (TPOs) are those that have institutionally distanced themselves from the political influence of government. Trade promotion requires a long-term strategy built on the experience of both private sector and public sector and the ability to respond quickly to market changes. This is the opposite of the short-term, noncommercial strategies usually adopted by many governments. Furthermore, in countries where political change can be significant, consistency can be achieved only by separating trade promotion from political influence. Australia and Costa Rica have both established political independence for their TPOs by structuring them as private public entities, managed by influential boards of directors, with a majority of votes from the private sector. These board members are elected for fixed terms and come from large and midsize exporters in a variety of industries. TPO status should state very clearly that the board, not the government, has final say over budget and policy issues. This helps to maintain a long-term private sector focus, regardless of the direction of political influences, leaving government-appointed directors to provide specialized expertise. Public sector directors in Australia and Costa Rica include high-level officials in the Ministry of Trade and other government departments. Representation from ministries of transportation, industry, science and technology, and even education is seen as desirable, given the role they all play in building a competitive export sector.

Costa Rica has given its TPO, Procomer, even more independence by linking its operating budget to export volumes through a US$3 tax on every export shipment. This provides an incentive to serve both large and small exporters, whereas an ad valorem levy would entice the TPO to concentrate on large companies and bulk product exports. Australia, on the other hand, recovers a substantial portion of its operating budget through user fees.

Other nations find it more practical to support TPO financial independence by blending multiple sources of funding. That way, user fees can be weighted toward the most export-ready companies, with other costs covered by an annual budget from the Ministry of Trade.

Can TPOs Use the Customer Relationship Management Approach?

An emerging best practice is a formal customer relationship management (CRM) system to track export results, assess client satisfaction for the information made available, and obtain constructive criticism. Australia does this as a component of its fee-based services system. Canada's Department of Foreign Trade (DFAIT) is upgrading its current client-tracking system with a sophisticated new virtual trade commissioner system that incorporates CRM. ProChile, Proexport (Colombia), and Procomer (Costa Rica) are among the most active TPOs in Latin America that have adopted CRM systems. CRM begins when a potential exporter first contacts a regional TPO office in the home country. From that point forward, the software-based system tracks their progress from first preparation to repeat sales. It identifies the exporter's training and facilitation needs, assesses their market-readiness, documents their first contact with a foreign market, and follows their participation in trade promotion events. Moreover, the system records the sales that exporters achieve over the first several years in a new market. These data allow the TPO to measure the return on investment of its various promotional activities so that it can constantly improve them. The private sector expression that "if you can't measure it, you can't manage it" also applies to the business of trade promotion.

Export Promotion Strategic Choices: The ProChile Example

Medium-sized emerging economies have more limited financial capacities than developed countries for carrying out national export promotion programs. Therefore, national authorities have no other choice but to limit the scope of their strategic objectives in selecting the industries with the best export potential.

Such an approach was chosen by Chile's export promotion agency, ProChile. This TPO was one of the first to make such difficult choices. Given Chile's geographical distance from so many of its export markets, ProChile understood that only a limited group of products could compete in global markets.

ProChile studied the competitive potential of its national industries and selected 10 sectors to be the core of its promotional efforts. As a direct consequence, hundreds of other industries were left with minimum or no support. However, today, Chile is recognized as a world export leader in those top 10 sectors, among others such as wine, fish, fruits and vegetables, lumber, and software. These successes were translated into employment growth and contributed to diversifying its past single-export base away from copper. Chilean export growth has been recorded as at the highest rate among all its neighboring countries in Latin America.

Regional/Sectoral Implementation of National Export Development Strategies

In large trading countries like India, new TPOs may exist either at the regional/state level (e.g., Karnataka TPO [http://www.ktpo.org], Tamilnadu TPO, or Chennai Trade Centre [http://www.chennaitradecentre.org]) or at the sectoral level (e.g., the information technology sector in India), showing clearly that implementing comparative advantages for export trade strategies at local/sectoral level can be developed, provided of course that the national export development strategy (NEDS) complies with the local/regional priorities.

In fact, some regions within countries—more or less with federal structures—are bigger (in terms of gross domestic product [GDP], export volume, natural resources, etc.) than many other individual countries in the world (e.g., the United States, Brazil, China, India). The federal state system allows local investments, resource allocations, and even taxes to be managed by the local authorities (e.g., United States, India), which in fact is an incentive for keeping benefits at the local level.

This trend will probably grow over time, given the information technology and infrastructure/institutional development and facilities in such countries, both in developed and in emerging economies. The only difference between the state and national/federal level is that multinational and bilateral trade agreements signed at the federal level are applicable at all state levels.

However, trade liberalization trends will influence the implementation of national export development programs. The World Bank estimates that by 2015 the continued reduction of tariffs on manufactured goods, the elimination of subsidies and nontariff barriers, and a modest 10% to 15% reduction in global agricultural tariffs would allow developing countries to gain nearly US$350 billion in additional income. Developed countries would stand to gain roughly US$170 billion. Such estimates, however, imply that successful schemes are adopted through the Doha Agenda or enlarged regional agreements.[1]

CHAPTER 7

Trade Promotion and Budget Allocation

Almost all trade promotion programs follow a similar path of assistance to the concerned exporter. It begins with assessing a company's readiness for export and proceeds through several phases, with the aim to conclude the firm's first export sales in the selected target market(s).

Considering the support provided by the trade promotion organization (TPO) throughout the process, this can be viewed as a large investment for the institution and company concerned, both from the human and financial resources viewpoint. Training and consulting are part of the continuous process of accompanying the company throughout the process. It may take months or years, depending on its export readiness. Planning and budget allocation over a medium- to long-term period is therefore crucial.

In planning the export promotion process, the TPOs must therefore build their programs with four key questions in mind:

1. In what industries and markets and to which companies are limited resources best allocated?
2. To what degree should the cost of the export promotion program be shared or financed by the exporter?
3. Which organizational/institutional structure is best suited to such trade promotion programs?
4. Which trade promotion initiatives provide the best results?

Based on the results gathered and agreed priorities, the resource allocation can be discussed.

A Crucial Budget-Allocation Task

The most challenging part of managing any budget is the allocation of limited resources among a large number of proposals, for the private as well as the public sector. Well-managed private companies strive to reinvest in their strongest divisions while cutting or dropping their weakest parts. In contrast, many trade promotion agencies, under political influences, tend to put their resources behind new or weak industries in the hopes of potential growth or in response to intense lobbying, as is the case in the agricultural sector.[1]

Some promotional agencies even avoid supporting the country's most competitive industries on the grounds that "they don't need our help." A case in point is Canada's original equipment manufacturer (OEM) auto-parts sector, one of the largest sources of Canadian exports, which receives disproportionately little marketing support from International Trade Canada. In fact, most TPOs are very careful not to be considered as aiding the nation's strongest companies.

However, when the results emerge, one can notice a rather low return on investment, particularly when a political approach to trade promotion is preferred to an economic-based strategy.

Focusing on a Few Markets

Today there are almost 200 countries in the world. The largest 25 countries represent 80% of global gross domestic production (GDP) and an even larger share of imports, which means that the remaining 175 or so countries represent less than 20% of the global export market.

For this reason, few of the world's largest companies try to penetrate more than 20 or 30 international markets. For example, Walmart, the world's largest private sector employer, operates in only 14 countries. General Electric, with an extensive international network, operates in only 59 countries worldwide. This raises the question of why so many countries operate full-scale export promotion offices throughout the world.

As stated earlier, traditionally trade promotion was an extension of the diplomatic infrastructure, carrying a political function. However, diplomacy has acquired a commercial focus for many countries, with most goals defined in economic, not political, terms. For this reason, countries that never built a global diplomacy network have the advantage of focus. Mexico's TPO, ProMéxico, operates in only 22 countries, with multiple offices in the largest markets. France, by comparison, maintains embassies in 166 countries, with significant commercial activity in most of them.

Does that mean that it is necessary to dismantle traditional infra-structures? It might be a pride-damaging process but not an impossible one. The United Kingdom's foreign service decided a few years ago to reduce more than a dozen offices in small Latin American and Caribbean nations and to centralize trade promotion activities in Miami, the region's trade center hub. British bureaucrats arrived at the same conclusion as their private sector counterparts: It is more cost-effective to service many of the region's small markets from Miami.

Downsizing in the Americas is just one of the cost-cutting measures that the United Kingdom took to bring down the high costs of trade promotion. According to a 2004 strategic paper on trade promotion authored in the United States, the United Kingdom spends more per export dollar on trade promotion than any other country.

Helping Those Who Can Help Themselves

Targeting specific foreign markets is a less controversial aspect of the notion of focus than the task of selecting which exporters or potential exporters will receive help and which will be turned away. Almost every country promoting trade likes to highlight its support for small and medium-sized enterprises (SMEs).

The motives are partly political, since they address an important and often disadvantaged constituency, but they are also pragmatic, in that they recognize that export sales can be a tremendous stimulus to build the next generation of corporate leaders.

SME support programs are often generous. The British Outward Missions Program provides travel grants up to US$1,500 for small busi-nesses to participate in a trade mission. The Netherlands and Australia have grant programs that pay for a substantial part of new exporters' costs (up to US$110,000 in the case of the Netherlands).

Unfortunately, most SMEs are not prepared to assume the full cost of servicing a new market, should they succeed in generating export sales. In most emerging markets where a large share of trade promotion is focused, market information is scarce, legal services can be expensive, product adaptation requires considerable time and expense, and intellectual property may not be well protected. Most companies spend US$150,000 to US$200,000 over 2 years to successfully introduce a new product line into a market. For companies approaching US$20 million in annual sales, this is a large but viable investment. For smaller companies, that kind of investment is too expensive. Yet in most markets, a US$20 million company is large.

Ironically, the highest ranking foreign trade promotion officer, an ambassador, normally reserves the bulk of his or her networking time for the benefit of the largest companies. Increasingly, the most valued service of an ambassador is the ability to open doors to key public- and private-sector enterprises in the host country for corporate interests. This is logical, since only the largest companies can readily take advantage of the opportunities derived from high-level diplomacy. There is no point to bid on the exploration of a new oil field and then send in a company that does not have the financial resource to submit a competitive bid.

When entering new markets, trade promotion officials would usually do better to design large and medium-sized enterprise (LME) programs, rather than those for smaller firms. It is the large companies that have the resources and staying power to really penetrate new markets. Once established, LMEs typically turn to their smaller suppliers to outsource their requirements for products and services.

Some trade promotion agencies, like Mexico's ProMéxico, recognize this dynamic and focus much of their SME promotion on linking small suppliers to large exporters, many of which may be foreign multinationals. Alternatively, SMEs should be encouraged to join forces in consortia-like groupings when pursuing opportunities overseas, pooling resources to finance the high cost of market entry.

Who Actually Pays Along the Path of Trade Promotion?

As far as the financial participation between the government (subsidies) and the exporter, the government funding is normally diminishing along the export process (from 100% to 0%), as long as new exporters move from educating themselves about foreign market opportunities to drafting and implementing a market-entry strategy, relying increasingly on export promotional costs that are tailored to their needs and for which they are prepared to pay for.

The basic steps will start with program awareness (seminars, booklets, Internet access, awards) and move to generic export readiness programs (in class or distance learning); customized export plan development, workshops, and practical experiences; identifying sales opportunities through trade missions, trade shows, opportunities matching, buyers missions, and so on; and closing market deals with in-market services.

The list of countries providing advice, information, or training related to export promotion at no cost to the exporter is definitely decreasing. The adage "people will only appreciate it if they have to pay for it" also applies to export promotion.

Most governments today try to share the cost burden of export promotion with exporters, especially as they require more customized services. The Australians begin with free access to their online database of export leads and provide initial consultations free of charge. But if SMEs need their help for opening markets, assessing distributors or setting up sales meetings, they should be prepared to pay modest to midlevel consulting fees for their services. The United States provides a list of prepriced services to assist with market entry. Chile's ProChile and Colombia's Proexport provide matching funds to export initiatives organized by industry associations, which in turn normally transfer the cost onto the participating exporter.

Some trade promotion professionals argue quite convincingly that SMEs require free services to help counter the many handicaps they face in global markets. Comparing two countries provides some insights. In Canada, a disproportionate amount of export promotion is directed at SMEs and very few user fees are levied. Though much of Canada's exports to the United States are dominated by the intracompany transfers of multinationals, Canada encourages its SME exporters to go it alone into overseas markets, where future opportunities exist. In spite of this, SMEs are responsible for only 9% of Canada's exports to the Asia Pacific region. In the United States, where user fees are immediately applicable on most services and few breaks are given to small businesses, SMEs generate 32% of all manufactured exports.

El Salvador is a smaller economy that restructured their export development agencies with the creation of Expro. Initial funding was provided by the U.S. Agency for International Development (USAID). Expro was designed to generate a sizeable portion of its budget from user fees.

Generally, sharing costs with exporters is a rather difficult task, particularly for the "old-school" agencies with large overheads and with long traditions of free public access. One industrialized country, which will remain unnamed, recently conducted an internal study to measure how much it would have to charge exporters if it converted to a full cost-recovery system. The result was the exorbitant figure of US$450 per hour. Many other export promotion agencies face the same problem: A shift to cost sharing would suddenly reveal just how constrained their budgets are. Obviously, they tend to resist undertaking such reforms.

As several countries have also learned, switching to user fees invites far more scrutiny and criticism from participating exporters. This forces TPOs to adopt more private sector–like practices such as surveying exporters for client satisfaction, focusing on markets and industries that provide good returns, and designing cost-effective promotion initiatives that are measured for their return on investment.

CHAPTER 8

The Exporter Profile

Making Exporting a Core Business

A recent study commissioned by the Australian government examined how seven developed countries are helping small and medium-sized enterprises (SMEs) enter export markets and maximizing the gains for such export activities. The study examined impediments to stronger export performance by SMEs and identified challenges that trade promotion organizations (TPOs) face in assisting the next generation of exporters.

The study, *Knowing and Growing the Exporter Community*, published by the Australian Trade Commission (Austrade; http://www.austrade .gov.au), classifies exporters and potential exporters into five categories:[1]

1. Nonintender
2. Intender
3. Accidental exporter
4. Global born exporter
5. Regular exporter

It then evaluates export promotion assistance programs and TPO initiatives by their ability to help each type of exporter with their specific export needs. This analytical framework focuses on the obstacles confronting each type of potential client and the tools that are appropriate for assisting them. However, the mix of issues faced by the exporter is somewhat different from one category to the next.

For example, Austrade concludes that 50% of new exporters are accidental exporters, who start into exporting because their clients are expanding abroad and ask them, as suppliers, to follow their business. Born global exporters are different kinds of companies: They are start-ups created with exporting in mind; they constitute another

25% of Australian new exporters. New exporters are less concentrated in traditional export sectors, more diversified, and more dependent on knowledge sharing. Only a quarter of new exporters are classified as successful intenders.

The decision to go into sustained exporting is often very demanding and uncertain. In the early stages of exporting, the risks a firm faces will rise sharply as it encounters new factors such as exchange rate exposure; long distances and time-zone differences; new modes of transport; new government regulations; new legal and financial systems; and different customers, requirements, and competitors. At the same time as the risks are rising, profitability is likely to fall as the firm invests in areas such as market research and development and working capital. Eventually risks can be expected to fall and profitability again rise, but that can be estimated as farfetched.

Similarly, a survey of Canadian exporters in 2010 gave the following final statement:

> Most new exporters start in a single market, usually with a single product. Thus, of the 13,164 new exporters in 2000, 96% started in one market and about two-thirds started in one market with a single product. Even as the number of new entrants plummeted to no more than 4,736 in 2006, these ratios remained stable, with the share of single market entrants falling only marginally to 92% and the share of single market and single product entrants rising marginally to about 71% over the period. The single most notable trend is the decline in the share of the exporter population accounted for by firms exporting to a single market and the associated rise of the multi-market (in most cases also multi-product) firm. In terms of firm size, we divide the Canadian exporter population into three groups:
>
> - the micro (1 to 10 employees),
> - small (11 to 50 employees), medium (51 to 200 employees), and
> - large (more than 200 employees).
>
> Most Canadian exporters belong to the micro and small size categories. Exporters of these two sizes made up almost four-fifths

of the exporter population. Large size exporters constitute a very small proportion of the total, around 5%. This size distribution did not change much from 1999 to 2006.[2]

With such a framework in mind, it is possible to organize best practices according to the role of the assistance program in moving clients from one level of export capability to the next (Table 8.1). Tables 8.2 and 8.3 illustrate specific exporter profiles for each category and the type of action required for each category. As outlined in Table 8.3, the first two types of initiative are usually delivered at home, the second two involve activities at home and abroad, and the final type is usually delivered abroad in the exporting market.

Table 8.1. Best Practices, Assistance Programs, and Levels of Export Capability

Categories (by growing commitment)	Nonwilling → Willing but not engaged → New exporter → Confirmed exporter
Type of action	Raising export awareness → Building → Export readiness → Selecting export target markets → Systematically identifying and exploiting export business opportunities

Table 8.2. Exporters Categories and Descriptions

Category	Description
Nonwilling or having limited intention	Not interested in exporting, usually because risks and costs are perceived as too high—sometimes the firm has a dominant or protected position in its own market and knows that its comparative local advantage is not working beyond the borders. (State trading companies or national service providers are the most frequent example.)
Willing but not engaged	Not exporting yet interested—such companies are still comparing the ratio cost/opportunity and start believing that exporting could be beneficial. They still don't know the real benefit of exporting.
New exporter with limited experience	Have completed at least one export sale but have not yet developed a regular export market—this category includes successful potential, ad hoc exporters, and born global exporters. Such companies are engaged in ad hoc operations
Experienced exporter	Enterprises with established export markets—they may come from the previous categories. They are already motivated about exporting and mainly seek more efficiency or expansion into new markets.

Table 8.3. Type of Action and Trade Promotion Tools Required

Capability/ awareness level	Initiatives	Specific trade promotion tool
Raising awareness (at home)	Initiatives are intended to raise awareness of the benefits of exporting and to provide a general understanding of exporting as a means of promoting nonwilling groups into willing exporters.	Market and product screening, global trade statistics (e.g., ITC Trade Maps) and desk research reports
Building export-readiness (at home)	Initiatives provide learning opportunities for willing groups to acquire the knowledge and skills necessary to become new exporters.	Training and awareness programs
Selecting target markets (at home and abroad)	Initiatives mainly help potential exporters identify and understand specific foreign markets/sectors where their products or services have good prospects enabling them to become new exporters. They also help experienced exporters move into new markets.	Desk and field research studies, trade information services
Identifying sales opportunities/building export trade channels (at home and abroad)	Initiatives inform potential exporters, new exporters, and experienced exporters about specific clients and their needs; expose products to buyers; and match exporters with potential buyers.	Inquiries, reply services abroad from trade representatives, Internet replies
Concluding and expanding export business (abroad)	These initiatives help potential exporters become new exporters and experienced exporters to expand their markets by helping them interact with prospective buyers, present offers, and complete export contracts. This category also includes follow-up services after the deal.	Field visits and promotional campaigns, trade missions organized through trade associations, trade representatives, participation in trade fairs, and Internet presence through Extranet networks

Assessing Export Capacities With an Export-Readiness Program

Some programs give more details on what to do in order to be prepared for the next export step. Best known among these tools is CORE, a program for assessing company readiness to export and decision-making support system.

Such a computer program was initiated in the 1980s as a self-evaluating system for a company considering export business based on its own "export readiness." The CORE program has been updated to the present environment, integrating new export information and communication techniques. It is a self-assessment tool that assesses a company's readiness to expand its operations internationally ("organizational readiness") and ascertains its ability to export a particular product. Based on the answers given to questions, it generates advisory statements and provides a "product readiness" statement.

CHAPTER 9

Trade Representation Abroad

A Key Component of Trade Promotion Strategy

The Key Functions of Trade Representation

A key link that any country must have in order to carry out an effective export promotion program is to have a network of active official commercial representatives posted abroad. These representatives may be career commercial officers or recruited from the business community for a fixed period on contract. In some cases, career officers of the diplomatic service may be responsible for commercial representation tasks.

Which Trade Representation Program and How Many?

Implementing a trade promotion program implies finding and entering more target countries to identify new partners abroad, assess the market potentials, understand the local rules and import regulations, participate in local trade fairs, assist business representatives, and so on—all basic activities that are facilitated by a trade representation office. The issue there, from a national point of view, is to decide (1) how trade representation will be implemented in foreign countries (how many offices should be opened), (2) what their status should be (public or not), (3) if they should operate as a separate entity (part or not of the national trade promotion organization [TPO]), or (4) if they should be integrated in the diplomatic representation.

The strategic decision to take (linked to the budget and resources available) may span from no participation or limited presence abroad to a widespread presence. To illustrate these issues, a global survey has been undertaken by the Inter-American Development Bank, whose results were summarized during the seventh World Conference of Trade Promotion Organizations, October 13, 2008.

> There is an important heterogeneity across countries in the region in terms of how agencies operate abroad. Some organizations have an extensive network of own offices abroad, whereas others just rely on their countries' diplomatic representations (embassies and consulates). Further, these representations do also exhibit substantial variation in terms of geographical coverage.[1]

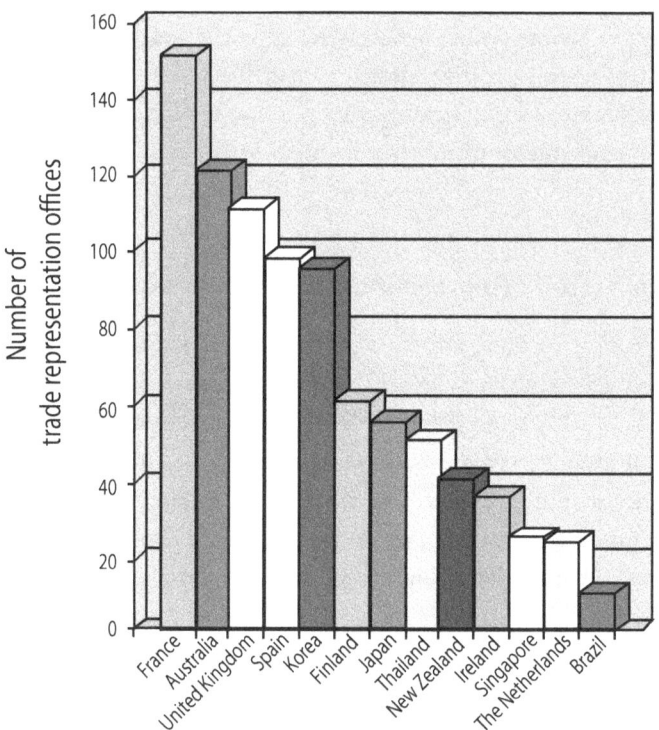

Figure 9.1. Number of countries with trade representation offices.

Source: Martincus (2008).

Impact of Trade Representation Versus Diplomatic Representation

In terms of impact made by export promotion organizations, the same report shows that their impact is significantly higher than the one registered by diplomatic representations. Trade representation offices report positive and significant impacts for a much larger number of export products than diplomatic representations offices. Trade promotion offices encourage diversification of exports of differentiated goods and services.

It also seems that opening a trade representation office has a substantially larger impact (5.5 times larger) on total bilateral exports than providing a series of services through an additional diplomatic mission. However, diplomatic foreign missions seem to contribute more to the expansion of homogeneous goods (commodities like maize, wheat, and copper).

Why These Results?

Organizational structure does seem to matter for the effectiveness of export promotion. In particular, the way trade promotion is organized abroad plays a role in explaining the impact on export results. It seems obvious that having specialized export promoting services abroad is the key to increasing export diversification. Specialized entities of TPOs are staffed with personnel who have proven experience in international marketing, and who are therefore capable of providing valuable assistance in exporting. In contrast, diplomatic missions do not always have a commercial section or personnel with the expertise needed to carry out the specialized function of export promotion. The mechanisms for coordinating TPO initiatives and foreign diplomatic missions are informal, weak, or even nonexistent. Officials formally responsible for export promotion usually lack career incentives for performing the required advisory activities and are also dealing with competing tasks.

However, TPOs do not necessarily have to open their own offices abroad. The same result could be achieved by strengthening trade competencies in diplomatic missions, increasing incentives for officials in charge with export promotion. But this requires addressing major institutional challenges. Sometimes, even, it is not possible in some countries where diplomatic missions are located in the nation's capital while the economic capital is elsewhere (e.g., Brazil, Turkey, India, Italy, Germany). If, as expected, the costs of these alternative strategies differ, a cost/benefit analysis will help to assess the best formula.

Integrating Trade Representation With Other Trade Promotion Activities Within a TPO

There is a trend toward integrating promotion activities (export, investment, business development, and in a few cases tourism) and trade promotion representation (and their foreign offices) in single organizations. France (through UBIFRANCE, the national TPO) recently made such a decision.

Another way to express this integration process is that TPOs should have their own offices abroad, but this raises the following questions:

- Should all diplomatic representations be equipped with commercial sections and relevant qualified personnel to perform the specialized task of export promotion? (If yes, the budget of those official representations would be much higher, taking in mind that they are financed mostly with public funding.)
- Are there incentives in the diplomatic structure that contribute to effective trade promotion activities?

France illustrates the first choice. In the French system, almost all countries have a diplomatic embassy representation with a trade commissioner office. The trade commissioner is an ambassador in charge of trade issues, seconded by specialized export-promotion officers (either civil servants or contractual staff, in specific key sectors). In addition, in major importing markets, professional and industrial associations may have their own promotion offices. This makes a rather large national public or semipublic expatriate community.

For the second choice, the question is clearly answered: The commercial function is completely integrated in the diplomatic structure, and in this case, incentives are low or nonexistent. However, in many countries (the United States among others), some interagency coordination persists, particularly among the Department or Ministry of Commerce and Ministry of Agriculture, regarding the allocation of overseas (specialized) staff for trade promotion activities. The agreement of each agency's roles and responsibilities in helping exporters is not easily reached.[2]

This issue is even more acute for small and medium-sized enterprises' (SMEs) assistance. The lack of detailed trade information data in foreign offices makes it difficult to assess progress or trends in SMEs' trade promotion activities across agencies.

Impact Evaluation: Trade Representation Using New Information Technologies

Trade representation abroad seems to help diversification of exports for companies, facilitating market penetration where the trade office is involved. To illustrate this point, an impact evaluation on trade assistance was undertaken in Peru: a survey made during a 5-year period (from 2004 to 2009) recorded a rate of growth of exports that was 17% higher for firms assisted by the Peruvian trade promotion office (PROMPERU), while those of the number of countries and the number of products were 7.8% and 9.9% higher, respectively. This implies that assisted firms would have a rate of growth of total exports 3.6% higher than nonassisted firms.

Export promotion has had a positive and significant effect on all these firm export outcomes. In particular, it has helped firms expand their exports through diversification of markets. The growth rate of exports per product is 7% higher for firms assisted by PROMPERU.

Trade information requirements tend to be more severe when entering a new market or starting to export a new product, as opposed to expanding operations on products already traded or in a country already served. Export promotion actions aiming at improving these trade information issues are more frequently considered as a priority area. In fact, for many TPOs, as well as trade representation offices, familiarity with information technologies (e.g., the Internet, websites, client and customer databases, social networks) is becoming essential, both for serving TPO clients (see case study 6 in part III, on Canadian virtual trade representation) and foreign partners.

An evaluation study compiled for the Canadian representation abroad in 2010 claims the following:

The impact of the programs delivered by the Canadian Trade Commissioner Service (TCS) on export performance by Canadian firms have been evaluated. A unique set of microdata has been created by linking three separate firm-level databases: Statistics Canada's Exporter Register and its Business Register, which provide information on export activity and firm characteristics, and the TCS client management database maintained by Foreign Affairs and International Trade Canada, which contains details on trade promotion services provided to Canadian firms. Data and information have collected to isolate the effects of public sector trade promotion.[3]

The Impact of Trade Commissioner Services (TCS) on Canadian Exporter Performance

It has been found that TCS programs have a consistent and positive impact on Canadian export performance. Exporters that access TCS services, on average, get 17.9 percent higher results in trade growth than those who do not. Furthermore, it was also found that TCS assistance benefits exporters in terms of product and market diversification.

—Johannes Van Biesebroeck, Emily Yu, and Shenjie Chen,
The Impact of Trade Promotion Services

Large exporters account for almost 70% of exports even though they made up only around 5% of the exporter population. A typical large Canadian export firm in the 2005–2010 period shipped about 18 products to about 7 markets, generating about Can$100 million in export revenues. By contrast, a typical medium-sized firm shipped about 7 products to 3 markets and generated only about Can$7 million in export revenues. Thus, in Canada, larger firms tend to export more products to more destinations and generate much higher export revenues than smaller firms.

Exporters that utilized the TCS have been more successful than those that did not. It can be seen that only about 5% of exporters each year sought assistance, while the propensity to seek TCS assistance increases steadily with the size of firm, rising from only about 3% of the microsized exporters to almost 17% of the large-sized exporters. More details are provided in case 6 in part III.

These findings are of the same magnitude and shape as those in many developed and developing countries or economies in transition. Unfortunately, few countries have undertaken satisfaction surveys or produced their results.[4]

As a conclusion, it seems that trade representation abroad is an effective function for trade diversification and positive impact when operating in host markets/countries. It seems also that these trade representation offices are better coordinated through the national TPO than through embassies. Finally, it seems that information technology and Internet communication networks play a growing if not key role in the effectiveness of such offices.

CHAPTER 10

Evaluation Practices

Once a trade promotion strategy has been adopted, and once the role of institutions by which the strategy is to be implemented has been defined, a key step still remains: the monitoring and evaluation phase. Monitoring and evaluation pose a number of challenges that need to be confronted, balanced, and solved. Experience shows that the most satisfactory solutions are in defining a monitoring and evaluation mechanism built into the strategy from the very begining.[1]

Considering the expected difficulties, is that process really useful? One obvious answer is that a credible monitoring and assessment mechanism will contribute to justify the resources put into the trade promotion program when reporting to financing authorities and stake holders.

More important are the expected benefits from monitoring and evaluation for all parties directly involved and those who benefit from its services. Assessment, when properly designed, organized, and implemented, enables policy makers to learn from the experience and increase the awareness in a manner that provides tools for refining the strategy.

In practice, planners will have to take into account the resources already spent and proposals for additional resources allocations; then they will have to learn through recorded feedback, which should be designed preferably from the start of the program. Unfortunately, practice shows that few countries or organizations evaluate the effectiveness of all their programs. Even fewer can claim they do it well (e.g., the United Kingdom Trade and Investment Board [UKTI] case in the second part of this book). What are the reasons for such a paradox?

Since evaluation aims to discover inefficiencies, the process frequently has negative connotations for participants. Moreover, the measures used are not always meaningful. Increased profit is a frequent quantitative measurement method, although evidence shows that such an increase is not always achieved in the short term. Other benefits realized through exporting, such as improvements in product quality or enhanced competitiveness in the domestic market, are not considered because of difficulties in quantifying them.

At the moment, there are a limited number of examples dealing with evaluation practices in the field of export promotion and development. Generally results are reported without sufficient coverage and clear methodology, providing few learning opportunities for examples cited. Nevertheless, despite these obstacles, a number of countries have placed evaluation at the focal point of their export promotion activities and are experimenting ways to get around.

Current practice in evaluation often focuses on specific activities, such as trade-fair participation programs, outward missions, advisory services, or seminars. There the most common approach is to evaluate the *overall performance* of participating companies. Generally the focus is on outcomes, and the criteria used are more often quantitative than qualitative (e.g., increased export volumes, number of new jobs created). The most frequently utilized information-collection methods are mail surveys or interviews.

Given the previously mentioned points, what are the important issues to consider when carrying out an evaluation?

1. *Consider both short- and long-term goals.* Trade New Zealand found, for example, that in some companies, benefits were still increasing beyond the first year of the export plan. In other cases, benefits may not be recorded until some time after the program has ended. For example, an increase in exports may be considered as a long-term objective, especially if the nonexporter or inexperienced exporter is targeted. It will take time for the participating companies to obtain an understanding of market needs, identify market contacts, and confirm the appropriateness of their export strategy.

2. *Identify the best component for measurement.* Although quantitative measures are generally favored, they are not always the most relevant. For example, a program providing subsidized participation at a trade fair may be aimed at nonexporters or new exporters with the objective of motivating them to consider exporting seriously for the first time. The most useful measure would discover the extent to which exporting is later viewed as a key part of the

company's overall strategy. In this case, using data of current sales or profit may result in a negative evaluation, even though the program is in the process of achieving its objectives.

3. *Service providers may change their activities according to the evaluation criteria to be used, in order to counterbalance negative statements.* Agents providing a service may focus on reaching fixed targets rather than applying the most relevant approach. For instance, deviation might arise when trade promotion officials may be tempted to improve results by targeting experienced exporters, who gained immediate results while ignoring the group of nonexporters or those new to the export business, who still have to expect positive results. To reduce such distortions, "softer" indicators such as contacts made and the number of agreements signed with distributors can provide a more useful measure. Further, an attempt could be made to evaluate changes in attitude toward exporting (using a survey of attitudes before the intervention as a base line) or to assess the extent to which the company's approach to exporting has become a long-term strategy. However, these concepts are much more difficult to quantify and may be less convincing, particularly if those in charge of evaluating the assessments prefer to consider "hard facts."

4. *Identify and consider only those results that have a direct relation to a specific activity.* The program should be evaluated by attempting to assess what would have happened without this activity. Evaluation of this component objectively requires an independant group approach. This, unfortunately, is rather the exception than the rule, the concerned institution preferring to conduct the survey by itself.

   For instance, a survey of matching samples is facilitated because a single trade promotion organization, is responsible for providing all offshore export promotion services to enterprises like ProChile. But in many countries, companies obtain support from a number of trade support institutions, there, control groups are difficult to identify. In such situations, alternative ways have to be found to isolate the impact of the program from the influence of other factors. New Zealand's approach tries to identify the proportion of companies' sales that can be attributed to the support received and asks companies to verify this.

Finally, vague objectives for export programs and unclear prior defini-
tions of effectiveness create problems as they make it difficult to identity
meaningful dimensions of impact. The lesson here is for implementing
agencies to ensure that all trade promotion programs have clearly specified objectives and success indicators.

A logical extension of the evaluation of specific programs is also to
undertake the evaluation of service providers. New Zealand and Ireland
provide two useful examples to evaluate the effectiveness of trade promotion programs:

1. Trade New Zealand (http://www.nzte.govt.nz)
   - Concentrate on impact: Determine foreign exchange gener-
     ated by clients and return on investment.
   - Keep client orientation: Focus on the achievement of a high
     deliver-in-full-and-on-time rating for specific services and
     try to reach a high customer-satisfaction rating.
   - Repeat the feedback exercise:
     o Compile monthly claims by account managers (e.g.,
       monthly)
     o Verify every 6 months by independent survey
     o Link performance results with resource allocation decisions
     o Schedule target settings
   - Measure achieved results at the level of sector team, the
     overseas commercial office, and the individual team
     members, with proper incentive to achieve targets (e.g., by
     payments).
2. Enterprise Ireland (http://www.enterprise-ireland.com)
   - Measure efficiency: Measure the costs of a particular promo-
     tional activity against reported foreign-exchange earnings.
   - Measure quality: Measure, through questionnaires to clients,
     the customer-satisfaction index for each service.
   - Analyze impact: Analyze the impact of the work performed
     on the business plan of the client.
   - Determine relevance: Determine the amount of fees gener-
     ated by a commercial office abroad.

Generally, the evaluation of trade services is performed in considering
the cost sharing by clients, whether the cost sharing is achieved by a fee

structure or by contributions based on value received. For example, Finland's FINPRO trade centers abroad are expected to cover up to one-fifth of their operating budget from fees. Individual assignments are evaluated for efficiency, quality, and impact, while individual trade officers are assessed on the basis of cost recovery and the extent to which they have become proactive marketers of their services.

Trade Promotion Strategies Evaluated at the Macroeconomic Level

Countries that have a national plan for export promotion are concerned in assessing its overall impact at national level. The evaluation criteria are, therefore, generally linked to the objectives driving a country's economic development.

Such objectives could be increased earnings of foreign exchange, employment creation, or poverty alleviation. However, attempts to demonstrate the link between achieved national performance (visible in national statistics) to the defined export promotion strategy itself is not obvious. Effective evaluation depends on reliable statistics with reliable data collection and management, exhaustive reporting by the custom authorities, by the national statistical services and by the central bank; if possible for developed countries, it could be a challenge for many developing countries!

Moreover, in the evaluation process, complex interactions may also raise a methodological challenge to isolate the attributable impact to a specific intervention.

For instance, a country that attracts investment from foreign companies will contribute to create a significant export output at the same time as it introduces measures to encourage indigenous small and medium-sized enterprises (SMEs) to export. Aggregate statistics showing an overall increase in foreign-exchange earnings may hide the contribution of the SME beneficiaries of the export promotion programs, or even more if these SMEs are not yet increasing their exports. On the other hand, indirect exports in the form of components or sub-assemblies supplied to the local affiliates of foreign multinationals by SMEs that have not benefited from export promotion programs may increase so significantly. The direct impact of export-promotion measures both for foreign companies and SMEs may not be correct for evaluation of the performance achieved.

Strategy Performance Indicators: The Philippines Case

The Philippines developed a strategy performance indicator to assess the impact of export on national development and the contribution of enterprises toward overall export expansion. Table 10.1 summarizes the indicators used.[2]

The impact on the national export strategy includes other factors, such as changes in the international environment. Growth in exports may be relatively easy to achieve when the global economy is also expanding but may be more challenging in a worldwide recession like in 2009. Sudden fluctuations in target markets can also have a rapid positive or negative effect on export performance (multiplier effect).

Internal mechanisms, institutions, and procedures that ensure effective implementation of strategies are also important. They include linkages and coordination among relevant organizations in both the public and private sector. Their absence may have a significant effect on impact. Similarly, a government commitment for exporting (that is clearly expressed to the business community) can contribute positively to improve the strategy performance. The opposite is equally true.

Table 10.1. Strategy Performance Indicators Used by the Philippines

Contribution to national development objectives	Contribution to enterprise growth and expansion of export base	Accomplishment of specific targets/initiatives
• National export performance • Percentage contribution of exports to gross domestic product (GDP) • Contribution of exports to new jobs created • Export growth by region	• Industry clusters formalized/established • Growth in value added of major export products • Net increase in number of exporters • Increase in number of export subcontractors and component suppliers • New export products developed and successfully launched	• Policy reforms achieved • Programs and services launched • Joint projects undertaken with other agencies • Bilateral/multilateral technical cooperation • Export-oriented livelihood programs launched

Source: Belisle (2000).

In addition, attention needs to be paid to the time lag between the initiation of a strategy and its implementation. The more sophisticated approaches tend to take a horizontal approach, for instance, to examine the implementation process in conjunction with the strategy itself and to draw conclusions taking into consideration other influencing variables. However, in the final analysis, it may be difficult to assess whether the impact is due primarily to the strategy itself or to the process (i.e., the strategy's design and implementation mechanisms).

Evaluation Focusing on Enterprise

Generally, when dealing with strategy making, it is important to look into the influence and impact of a national export development strategy (NEDS) from the company point of view, considering both the process and outcome. Evaluating the process then consists in understanding the way a company views the NEDS, how it takes advantage of any trade promotion programs offered, and how the support received is integrated within the company existing activities. At that stage, it can or cannot turn into outcomes. The evaluation is then an attempt to analyze the extent to which these outcomes have been generated, or at least influenced, by the NEDS and its associated programs.

But obstacles raise up at individual company level when linking an impact directly to a specific action or experience, like participation to a specialized trade fair. The same environment can be perceived differently by companies depending on their experience. For some firms, such participation will be perceived as a fresh new experience, while for others, it could just be strengthening or continuing on an already familiar export market or assessing the market with their own agents.

This drives results in different levels of awareness of, attitudes toward, and utilization of specific export development initiatives. It means that firms that appear at the first glance to be similar are likely to take different decisions regarding their future export activities.

As a result of these factors, given the presence of so many variables, the validity of claims that every dollar spent on export promotion has led to an increase of X dollars in exports seems at best questionable, given the influence of external factors like the global economic situation, political factors, and so on. All these findings tend to reinforce the idea that there are no ideal approach. In fact, each national strategy needs to be assessed within its own particular context.

That means the trade officials should take into account the main levels (enterprise, program, service provider, and macroeconomic environment) when designing and implementing export promotion programs. Despite these difficulties, it still can be possible to develop a specific approach to evaluate the NEDS.

Such approach should start at *enterprise* level and its needs. Existing resources and local business conditions clearly influence business capacity to understand and benefit from the proposed support and advisory services. The impact of an overall export promotion strategy is definitely linked to the perception and understanding of the proposals made to the firms.

The next levels concern the evaluation of *programs* and assessment of *service providers*, respectively. As illustrated previously, it is there that one can find most of the information about practices.

Finally, the macroeconomic environment level to consider for evaluation is where all levels are integrated and considered in the whole context of the wider national environment. There, the international regulatory environment (e.g., provided by the World Trade Organization [WTO]) and the political stability of the country concerned, the government's long-term commitment to supporting exporters, all are important influences to take into consideration.

Definitely, at each level of evaluation,[3] it is important to turn to both *process* and *outcome*, irrespective of whether the purpose of evaluation is reporting on impact of a given program to a funding institution (*static process*) or an internal review of the program for refining it during the course of implementation (*dynamic process*). It is clear that increasing attention should be given to the dynamic process, implying ongoing assessment—both qualitative and quantitative. Such attention definitely feeds into a better management process.

As a concluding remark, the capability and level of cooperation within the network of organizations involved are key determinants of what can be achieved in the evaluation process, as well as the availability of finance to implement trade promotion strategies.

The Future of Trade Promotion

Globalization has revolutionized the way business is conducted in recent years, and there is every indication that it will continue to do so, despite the 2008–2009 world financial crisis. In fact, the world trade environment is generating new requirements affecting markets:

- The widening trade liberalization is favoring the emergence of new trading patterns (e.g., supply chains becoming constantly appraised by buyers) that are likely to influence future trade flows.
- The international marketplace is being increasingly influenced by real-time information and communication systems. Markets/clients are becoming more specialized, more efficient, and ultimately more demanding of the suppliers.

It is essential to organize an integrated competitive response for the trade promotion strategy developers engaged in the globalization process.

A global competitiveness-based approach to trade development must replace the traditional market-based focus that many trade promotion organizations (TPOs) continue to pursue, possibly influenced by their traditional clients, if not by the national institutions involved in trade promotion.

Globalization has introduced another challenge for the TPOs: to ensure that export performance makes a significant contribution to overall economic development, despite the fact that a higher percentage of exports on the gross domestic product (GDP) means more dependency on foreign markets. Many countries do not have the size or domestic potential of China or the United States.

Complementary Objectives

In fact, competitiveness and development objectives do not contradict themselves; they can be driven in parallel. Together, they ensure long-term, sustained improvement in export performance, but their compatibility does not come per se.

Another challenge confronting national TPOs is how to make them complementary to the work undertaken by other national institutions or private sector representatives. What does this mean for TPOs?

1. TPOs must *be more comprehensive* in their approach. Competitiveness-based export-development assistance requires that trade support should be available to the business community at all critical points of the export value chain. Support must be made available to exporters to help them produce better products/services, communicate rapidly with existing or potential markets, and deliver more competitively. Furthermore, support must be available to new entrepreneurs and even to new export-oriented nongovernment organizations (NGOs).

2. TPOs must *specialize*. Providing general services does not contribute to improved competitiveness. Specialized services do. The range of specialized services needed to sustain export competitiveness at the national level and the new investment linked to such a specialization are beyond the capabilities of a single trade support organization. A multiple-agency approach to export development is required.

3. TPOs should *build a national trade support network* with other institutions involved in the export development process, including with the private sector. They must strengthen their network through partnerships, both domestic and abroad. TPO officials must reinforce such networks by implementing joint programs with other specialized trade support organizations, ideally focusing on a specific and identified need within the export community.

4. All the network members must keep on top of a fluctuating business environment by *being prepared to adapt*. TPOs must benchmark their performance, measure results, and adjust when the impact is less than planned.

From these requirements, four tracks emerge:

1. *Establish a unifying vision for all members of the network.* This step implies the preparation of a national export development strategy (NEDS), primarily based on a realistic assessment of medium-term export opportunities, the constraints to achieving a competitive advantage, and the strengths and resource limitations of key members of the national trade support network. The defined strategy is put in place with the full participation of other network members, including ongoing political endorsement.

2. *Ensure that every network has a catalyst and a coordinator.* The national TPO is best qualified to undertake both roles and should take the lead to
   - identify the elements of a competitiveness-based approach to export development,
   - determine the areas where trade can best contribute to overall economic development,
   - create a national trade support network that involves public-private sector partnerships.

3. *Maintain the TPO as the focal point.* The national TPO should be the first point of contact for the individual exporter (see the part III case studies). Focus on providing the three basic but essential specialized services to all network members and enterprises involved: commercial intelligence, export counseling, and hands-on referral services.

4. *Enlarge and expand networks at regional level.* Other multilateral development organizations, such as the World Bank and regional development banks, can assist in this process of repositioning TPOs. They may include TPOs in their efforts to insert export promotion activities into national economic development. In the 1980s, some development agencies had become highly critical of the performance of many TPOs among others in developing

countries (but not exclusively), some of which needed improve-ments. Since that time, many more have become competent and efficient. Today, definitely, TPOs are prime national players for ensuring that trade is an effective engine for development.

In fact, those who show the path are nominated and rewarded in the TPO Network Conference organized by the ITC, which began in 2000: the World TPO network Awards (http://www.tponetwork.net). In recent years, a number of countries have applied new tools for the implementation of their trade promotion strategies. While some of the experiences are easily transferable, others may need more substantive efforts to reach comparable results. Ultimately the aim is to provide practical and workable ideas to other TPOs. This will constitute the following parts II and III of this book, which describe the best tools and practices considered by the profession.

PART II

Best Practices

Tools, Functional Cases, and Sectoral Cases

CASE 1

Identifying and Finding Markets for Trade Promotion

Websites and Trade Statistics/ Market Analysis Tools*

Trade promotion organizations (TPOs), over the last few years, have built and maintained Internet access through web portals. The main goal is to optimize and present trade information services and resources produced at national or international level. In fact, national TPOs generally have set themselves as trade information resource centers for finding trade data or opportunities in their own country. Many of these TPOs are offering information on their own national environment, regulations, procedures, and so on. Others offer more services online, accessible not only to nationals but also to foreign visitors, and in this they illustrate the most recent trends in client orientation, which hopefully will probably be followed by other information providers.

Examples of Trade Information Given by TPOs

National Level

Three web portals have been bookmarked and awarded by other web information providers:

1. Austrade (http://www.austrade.gov.au)
2. New Zealand Trade and Enterprise (http://www.nzte.gov.nz)
3. UK Trade and Invest (http://www.ukti.gov.uk)

---

*This case was prepared by Ms. Aurora Mendez, graduate assistant at International University in Geneva.

They all show a global approach:

- Excellent customer orientation, profiling, and customization of information and services to different users, with concern about the client's profiles
- High quality of the information provided, with efficient advice on how to select and present data
- Easy integration of various and cross-referenced components (e.g., information, help, tools) with widely used social media (Facebook, YouTube, Twitter)
- Easy to subscribe add-in services like newsletters and alert systems

It should be mentioned that these websites are open to any user without restriction (no password or prior registration needed). At the moment, they represent the best interface for users and visitors at national level.

International Level

International trade organizations are offering a large range of information, not always accessible for nonregistered users. The following international trade organizations have their own websites, which reflect their main activities with their specific profiles:

- The International Trade Centre (ITC; http://www.intracen. org) has a wide range of statistical data accessible (but not all tools are for free), see the following case study.
- The World Trade Organization (WTO; http://www.wto.org) is focusing on trade rules and regulation (with a large database).
- The United Nations Conference on Trade and Development (UNCTAD; http://www.unctad.org) provides data on international trade, commodities, and investment issues. See the cotton case in part II, case 3 developed further.
- The World Bank maintains an integrated database on trade issues, jointly developed with the previously mentioned organizations, called the World Bank Integrated Trade System (WITS; http://wits.worldbank.org).

This subject of trade information sources and access is a very large one and would exceed this book's purpose. However, the previously mentioned websites are a good image of what can be expected with the information technology and communication tools from a trade promotion strategy point of view.

From such best-practice findings, it is easier to trace the features of the future Internet access facilities: interactivity with the user's needs (national or foreign) and on-profile building advice (e.g., the Canadian Virtual Trade Commissioner, developed further in part III, case 6). At the end of this case, a list of some TPO web addresses is provided.

Market Analysis Tools for Trade Promotion Developed by the ITC

The ITC has been an established provider of international trade statistics through the COMTRADE (Commodity Trade Statistics) database, created and maintained in partnership with the United Nations Statistical Office (UNSO). Beyond the statistics, the ITC is offering a wide range of market-analysis tools developed in close partnership with international trade institutions (e.g., UNCTAD, WTO, the World Bank, nongovernment organizations [NGOs]) and national institutions. Each market-analysis tool serves a specific analysis purpose; however, the combination of all of them can offer the user, either public or private, a sound understanding of domestic and global markets over a quite large product range—over 5,300 products—by country, sector, or region.

These tools, called *maps*, have complementary purposes. For instance, *Trade Maps* allows for the understanding of world demand and the detailed or global analysis of trade flows. *Investment Map* helps the user to identify sources of foreign direct investment (FDI) and to identify present and potential competitors. Moreover, *Mac Map* reflects changes in market access conditions and displays market access barriers. Finally, *Trade Competitiveness Map* allows policy makers, businesses, and TPOs to benchmark a country's sectoral performance and define a trade strategy according to the country's situation.

In this context, to quote an official trade promotion operator, Stanley Theard of the Ministry of Commerce and Industry in the Caribbean region argues that "these market and product analysis tools have responded to one of the Ministry of Commerce and Industry's major pre-occupations with regard to achieving a better mastery of information in order to have strategically oriented investment activities for the production of goods and services in our country."[1]

Even though these tools are also used by developed nations, they are oriented to help developing countries to define a strong trade promotion strategy. The main reason behind this is that most companies in developing countries are small and medium-sized enterprises (SMEs) and often lack the resources to invest in expensive market analysis or benchmarking activities. National trade promotion institutions can therefore support SMEs in this situation and help them to develop their commercial potential in domestic and international markets.

The ITC's tools provide trade data, information, and different types of analyses to TPOs, enterprises, policy makers, and governments, with the following goals:

- Understand some of the main trends in the current global trade environment.
- Facilitate trade analysis.
- Help businesses, TPOs, and policy makers to develop a comprehensive and competitive export strategy.
- Engage in local and international networks to deliver support to more businesses.
- Promote the cooperation between the private and the public sectors in the development of long-term strategies to boost economic growth and trade.
- Ensure that small and medium business priorities are integrated into domestic trade policies.

The ITC delivers these tools counting on a multiplier effect, where experts organize workshops to train policy makers, government officials, or even exporting companies so they can spread their knowledge in their respective institutions and countries.

At this time, the ITC has four tools that focus on specific areas of international trade, identification of markets/products, as well as on the attraction of FDI. However, as mentioned previously, these tools are complementary to each other, and the combined use of them helps businesses, policy makers, and governments to strategically conduct business in the competitive global trading environment. To better understand how they relate to each other, they are described in more detail in the following sections.

Trade Map

Understanding the structure and evolution of international markets is crucial to both companies and TPOs in order to develop a comprehensive and solid export strategy. Trade Map aims to provide strategic market research by monitoring both the domestic and international performance of specific products, raising awareness of the comparative and competitive advantages, identifying the potential for markets and products diversification, and designing and sorting by priority business-development programs for both companies and for trade support institutions.

Trade Map provides indicators of market and product performance, demand, alternative markets, as well as the role of competitors. This tool also displays information in boxes and tables and allows the user to obtain information based on regional groups of countries and products.

Using these maps, TPOs can set priorities regarding issues such as trade promotion, sectoral performance, partner countries, and trade strategies to use resources more efficiently. The types of questions that can be addressed are linked to strategic market research with detailed statistical information on international trade to identify priority products and markets. They provide answers to the following types of questions:

- What is the size of the world market for a product?
- What are the trends for that market (i.e., is the market growing and by how much)?
- With which countries does my country currently trade for certain products?
- Are there opportunities to identify new or alternative markets?
- What tariff barriers exist in a specific market?
- What are my country's priority products and markets for trade promotion?

- What countries supply the majority of my country's imports?
- What alternative sources of supply are available?
- What is my country's current trade performance?
- For what products is there potential to increase bilateral trade with a specific partner?
- What are the trade flows between my country and a specific region or economic group?
- What are the most recent export/import trends of a product?
- Which countries compete to supply to a specific market and to the world?[2]

The information contained in Trade Map is based on the largest database of trade statistics in the world, COMTRADE, which is maintained by the United Nations Statistical Office (UNSO). According to ITC experts, COMTRADE covers more than 90% of the world trade. This allows Trade Map to include more than 220 countries and territories and 5,300 products defined at a level of 2, 4, or 6-digits in the harmonized system.

In addition, Trade Map contains information on tariff barriers for more than 40 countries for a 5-year period and provides detailed information on the conditions to access bilateral markets for all products and countries, including specific tariffs and ad valorem quotas and bilateral and regional agreements.

Trade Map helps different users to perform the following activities:[3]

- *Analyze existing export markets.* This function examines the performance and dynamics of export markets of a country for any product, identifies the number and size of export markets and export concentration, and highlights the countries where market share has increased.
- *See competitors in the global market.* This tool classifies competing countries that export the same product in terms of value, with additional indicators of quantities and market-share growth. It also highlights the position of a country in the world exports, as well as the position of other countries with respect to one market or product.
- *Evaluate competitors in specific export markets.* This assesses a country's competitors in any target market, with information

on the export performance of these competitors, and shows the number of supplying countries and their market performance.

- *Find information on barriers to market access.* This function provides information at the tariff line on the main instruments used to control the trade of the countries, such as ad valorem and specific tariffs, most-favored-nation (MNF) tariffs, quotas, and bilateral and regional agreements.

- *View trade data at the tariff line.* Trade flows are described at the most detailed level for an average of 10,000 products and over 80 countries worldwide, covering nearly 90% of world trade.

- *Identify new sources of supply.* Countries that export a product to the world as well as to a specific country are ranked against one another, allowing direct comparisons of actual and potential sources of domestic supply.

- *Study the opportunities for product diversification in a specific market.* A comparative assessment of the import demand of related products in a given market can be done. The user can also identify whether similar products are being imported by the country studied and whether synergies are possible.

- *Assess the country's trade performance.* A general assessment of the country's trade performance can be done, as well as the identification of priority areas for trade promotion and investment at a sectoral and product level.

- *Identify existing and potential bilateral trade with any country partner or region.* Bilateral trade opportunities can be identified by comparing actual bilateral trade and demand in terms of global imports of partner countries and the overall offer capacity of the country of origin.

Investment Map

International trade and FDI, traditionally perceived as different means to penetrate markets, have both witnessed a strong growth since the beginning of the 1980s. A combination of different factors can explain the tremendous growth of international trade investment. These include reductions in custom duties and transport costs as well as political events, such as the inclusion of Eastern Europe and Central Asia and their transition to market economies, as well as the strong development induced by regional integration.

Definitely, FDI and international trade are becoming increasingly complementary and are creating new business opportunities. The reasons that may be behind the positive relationship between FDI and trade flows can be summarized as follows:

1. Exports may encourage FDI flows to recipient countries of exports as a first step in the internationalization of the exporting companies.
2. Imports simultaneously encourage FDI inflows in the recipient country.
3. Exports may also encourage FDI inflows of foreign companies seeking externalities resulting from concentrations.
4. FDI outflows increase imports based on vertical integration.
5. FDI inflows can promote exports since many companies change their location (lower costs, cheaper resources, etc.) to export to the issuing country of FDI.

In this context, trade and FDI promotion activities must be undertaken jointly or at least in a coherent manner. This explains why in about 15 countries trade and FDI promotion activities are both undertaken under the supervision of a single institution.

Considering the clients' needs, investment promotion agencies (IPAs) are faced with the following questions from the *Investment Map User Guide* quote:

- Which sectors have a strong potential to attract FDI in my country?
- Which are the promising sectors in terms of export-platform FDI or which present interesting prospects for import substitution?
- Which countries are my main competitors at attracting inward investment in sectors in which my country has potential? Which rival countries have had the most success at attracting foreign investment in their country's potential sectors?
- Which foreign companies could invest in my country in particular sectors or products?

- What are the main companies active in the subregion or in my competitors' country?
- Where are the foreign companies located? Where are their headquarters?
- What are their contact details?[4]

To help answer these questions, Investment Map provides a tool that combines FDI data, trade flow data, and tariffs. In response to users' needs, company data on foreign affiliates located in developing countries has recently also been included.

Investment Map is also intended to assist IPAs to identify potential sectors for FDI and to target groups of investors.

An understanding of a country's strengths and weaknesses is essential for IPAs and TPOs. Today's markets are marked by strong international competition for FDI. As such, the targeting of potential sectors and investors is crucial for IPAs because it enables them to better manage their resources and to concentrate their efforts on potential investment channels. The public and private sectors may benefit from Investment Map, as it enables them to do the following:

- Identify potential investment projects targeting regional and international markets.
- Better focus on identifying the constraints on export development in certain markets caused by high tariffs and hence serve as a guide for future trade negotiations.
- Provide a benchmark of their competitiveness.
- Give advice concerning the improvement of the investment and business environment.[5]

Investment Map's primary assets are its considerable geographical coverage; its combination of FDI, trade, and tariff data; and its information on foreign affiliates. Investment Map displays the following information:

- Total FDI flows and stocks for approximately 200 countries and territories
- FDI flows and stocks organized by industry (International Standard Industrial Classification [ISIC] revision 3) for approximately 80 countries

- Data on exports and imports, as well as indicators on trade potential for approximately 180 countries
- Data on the tariffs applied by over 170 countries and the data on tariffs faced by over 200 countries and territories
- Information on the location, sales, employment, and parent company for over 70,000 foreign affiliates operating in developing countries or in transition economies (for 1,000 business lines classified under the Standard International Trade Classification [SITC]).[6]

The FDI data are taken from the UNCTAD's database, which is updated several times a year, and some data are also collected directly by ITC experts.

Market Access Map

In order to design a comprehensive trade strategy, it is essential to know the market access conditions, as well as the import tariffs applied by the target markets. Equally, businesses are constantly looking to diversify their products, markets, and suppliers. Therefore, the relevant questions are as follows:

- What are the customs duties that my products will face in other countries?
- What are the countries that provide favorable conditions for market access for my product?
- Where are the opportunities for market diversification?
- What are the tariffs faced by my competitors?
- Where can I obtain sources of raw material to get the greatest benefit from preferential trade agreements and free trade agreements signed by my country?[7]

Strategic market research includes a detailed analysis of the conditions of market access and trade on the international level. To that purpose, the Market Access Map helps the TPOs evaluate business performance and identify priority products and markets for commercial development by answering the following types of questions:

- What are the priority products and markets to promote trade with another country?
- In what areas does my country have a competitive advantage in regard to market access?
- Is my country taking full advantage of preferential access to certain markets?
- What are the countries that supply the majority of the goods imported by my country?
- Can my country import from other providers to minimize import tariffs?[8]

Furthermore, it is noteworthy that the needs of trade policy makers and trade negotiators differ slightly from those of the TPOs and businesses. The former not only need an overview of the tariff profile of their country and the tariffs their products will face in key markets but also need to understand the situation of other countries. In other words, both need to understand their countries' current position compared to that of other countries with which they have commercial activities. They must also anticipate future changes in the status quo and identify which situation is the most favorable one.

On the other hand, trade policy makers and trade negotiators, especially those of developing countries, must be able to answer questions such as the following:

- Is my country being adversely affected by trade barriers?
- What are the ad valorem equivalents of specific tariffs that my country has to face?
- What is my country's position versus its competitors from the perspective of the real level of protection faced in key markets?
- Is my country at such risk that its preferential access to key markets will be affected if key markets reduce their tariffs (MFN) for certain products?
- What are the most sensitive products and markets in my country in the current trade negotiations?
- What are the modalities for tariff reduction that would favor my country in the current trade negotiations?

- Which countries would benefit my country in a free trade agreement?[9]

Market Access Map aims to provide strategic research issues related to market access and competitive advantages, identify the potential for diversification of products or markets, prioritize business development programs, and prepare a country's position in commercial negotiations. Market Access Map allows users to do the following:

- Identify the tariff applied to a product by one country at the national tariff line.
- View preferential trade agreements and preferential rates applied by a country to another.
- Check the rules of origin of a preferential trade agreement.
- Compare global tariffs applied by all countries to a product exported by the country.
- Compare tariffs that your product faces vis-à-vis the tariff applied to competitors in any given market.
- Review tariffs applied by one country to all products exported by the country.
- Create product groups or countries to calculate average tariffs.
- Simulate tariff reductions on bound tariffs by using a standard formula for tariffs reduction or by using your own formula.
- Assess the actual levels of protection using ad valorem equivalents calculated by Market Access Map for all specific applied tariffs.[10]

Market Access Map covers 170 countries' applied tariffs on products exported by 239 countries and territories. Products are described at the most detailed national tariff line.

Trade Competitiveness Map

Trade Competitiveness Map (known as Country Map) provides country market analysis profiles for around 240 countries and territories. Each profile provides a series of tools to facilitate strategic market research, monitor national and sectoral trade and macroeconomic performance, and design trade development strategies.

For each country, Trade Competitiveness Map offers the following:

- *Trade performance index (TPI).* This assesses sectoral trade performance. The TPI provides a general profile and ranking for a country's key export sectors as well as a series of static and dynamic indicators to assess each sector's international competitiveness. Five years of trade data are provided.
- *National export performance and national import profile.* This provides an overview of the export/import performance of countries by looking at the composition of their trade portfolio in terms of the dynamics of international demand and sector diversification. Five years of trade data are provided.
- *The consistency of trade statistics and technical notes on trade data.* This provides a comparison of a selected country's trade statistics with partner country statistics in order to identify discrepancies between the two and gauge their consistency. Technical notes provide comments on the way national trade data has been gathered and on its limitations.

Useful Links

International Trade Centre, "Trade Map Trade Statistics for International Business Development" (http://www.trademap.org)

International Trade Centre, "Guided Tour and User Guide" (http://www.trademap.org)

International Trade Centre, *Investment Map User Guide* (http://www.investmentmap.org/docs/invmap-userguide-en.pdf)

Market Access Map, *Market Access Map—User Guide: Making Tariffs and Market Barriers Transparent* (http://www.macmap.org/User.Guide.aspx)

CASE 2

Market Analysis Tools in the Context of Mexican Foreign Trade*

Overview

Mexico is a country that over the past 6 decades has been guided and structured, in their productive activities and foreign trade, by 3 sets of systems or policies in the economic field:

1. From 1950 to 1972, the economy maintained a system that was called "industrialization via import substitution."
2. From 1972 to 1981, the political system showed a strong state involvement in the economy.
3. From 1982 to date, the system or set of policies has focused on "trade and economic liberalization" aimed at the insertion of Mexico into the global economy.

During the last 10 years, Mexico has undertaken the important task of trade liberalization. This has allowed Mexico to become a trading power and a key player in international trade. Today, Mexico has several free trade agreements that provide secure access to preferential markets in 32 countries in 3 continents, with a potential access to 61% of the world's gross domestic product (GDP).

Exports are the most dynamic sector of the Mexican economy and the first generator of employment. In recent years, exports have contributed

---

*This case was prepared by Ms. Aurora Mendez, graduate assistant at International University in Geneva.

to more than half of the national GDP growth. Due to this, Mexico has achieved the following:

1. It has become the 16th exporter in the world and the first in Latin America, surpassing countries like Spain, India, Taiwan, Malaysia, Chile, Australia, and Brazil.
2. It is the only country in the world to have preferential access to markets in North America, western Europe, and Latin America.

However, despite the great advances of Mexico in foreign trade, there are still outstanding tasks to be performed. One of them is to increase the participation of Mexican products in markets the country already supplies, like the United States, Europe, and Latin America, and to diversify the Mexican exports portfolio to new emerging and growing markets.[1]

Alignment of the Government, the Private Sector, and Other Institutions in the National Exports Promotion Strategy

One of the top priorities of the Mexican government has been to create the necessary conditions for national companies to grow and have access to international markets. For this reason, the government has taken actions aimed at achieving a stable macroeconomic environment, improving the national infrastructure and creating an institutional framework that gives certainty to domestic and foreign entrepreneurs.

The export promotion strategy includes the creation of working groups involving federal and state governments, the private sector, and specialized agencies to promote the use of trade and investment opportunities offered by free trade. These groups will be the commercial intelligence networks that, depending on their areas of competence and expertise, will operate at the national, international, sectoral, and regional levels.

The international network is composed of representatives of government agencies like the Department of Foreign Affairs, the Ministry of Economy, the national foreign trade bank (Bancomext), and Mexico's trade promotion organization (TPO; ProMéxico), as well as business executives and members of chambers of commerce. All of these will carry out tasks such as the identification of the demand for Mexican products in existing and new markets. Within Mexico, the national network consists of the Secretariat for Small and Medium-Sized Enterprises (SMEs), the Secretariat of Economic Development, Bancomext, and business organizations who will determine the exports supply by identifying current and potential exporters as well as the characteristics of their products. This network organizes regional, sectoral, and international forums to promote international trade and investment opportunities.

Evolution of the Mexican TPO to Address the Challenges

The government of Mexico launched a program called the "National Development Plan 2007–2012," which was intended to improve the Mexican economy and foster international trade. The plan's implementation had significant and beneficial impacts at the international level as well as on foreign direct investment (FDI) in Mexico.

As a part of this plan, the former secretary of economy announced on March 14, 2007, the creation of ProMéxico, a new agency for the promotion of Mexican foreign trade, national markets, and investment. It is important to mention that while ProMéxico is an autonomous federal institution due to its nature, it is an integral part of the National Development Plan 2007–2012.

ProMéxico can be seen as a promotional entity for marketing and the opening of new markets as well as the promotion of foreign trade and investments. It is intended to encourage the internationalization of Mexican companies to contribute to the economic and social development of Mexico. It also supports the promotional activities of the National Development Plan in order to make Mexico the Logistic Platform of the Americas.

ProMéxico will finance projects designed to open new markets and market niches for Mexican products and services and promote foreign trade and investment. This entity started up with a federal budget of 800 million pesos (US$75 million in 2007) and has been increasing its budget yearly.

Before the creation of ProMéxico, assistance to Mexican firms regarding foreign trade was an activity carried out by Bancomext, the Mexican bank for foreign trade. Bancomext has especially assisted SMEs to increase their presence in global markets by providing advice, financing, and promotional services. Bancomext will keep on supporting SMEs by granting productive financing, and NAFINSA (Nacional Financiera) will provide the advisory for the development of financial services to micro, small, and medium-sized companies that carry out export activities.

ProMéxico's headquarters are based in Mexico City. However, it operates through a network of 52 offices throughout the country and 35 offices in 19 countries. Through its offices, ProMéxico is highly linked to business and trade promotion agencies all over the world.

Meeting Mexico's Product Supply and International Demand

This new approach of exports promotion implemented under the National Development Plan 2007–2012 arises from the identification of market opportunities for Mexican products according to two criteria: First, it is important to identify products that Mexico's trading partners import from third parties, which do not enjoy the tariff preferences Mexico has to offer, and second, it is also important to promote the exports of products that, despite not having a relative preference, can compete in the international arena due to their price, quality, and proximity to potential markets.

Figure C2.1 shows the export value of each product (size of the bubbles) and compares Mexico's annual increase in world market share since 2005 (horizontal axis) with the annual growth of international demand between 2005–2009 (vertical axis). This chart shows the export performance in dynamic terms.

As can be seen, Mexico has lost world market share in exports of products such as mineral fuels, organic chemicals, beverages, plastic and articles, and so on. These industries and their products can be identified with the light grey shaded bubbles. Some reasons behind this loss could be the increasing Chinese exports to Mexican main trading partners such as the United States and the European Union. Mexico has not been able to compete with the prices offered by Chinese products and has been slowly substituted as a supplier of these products.

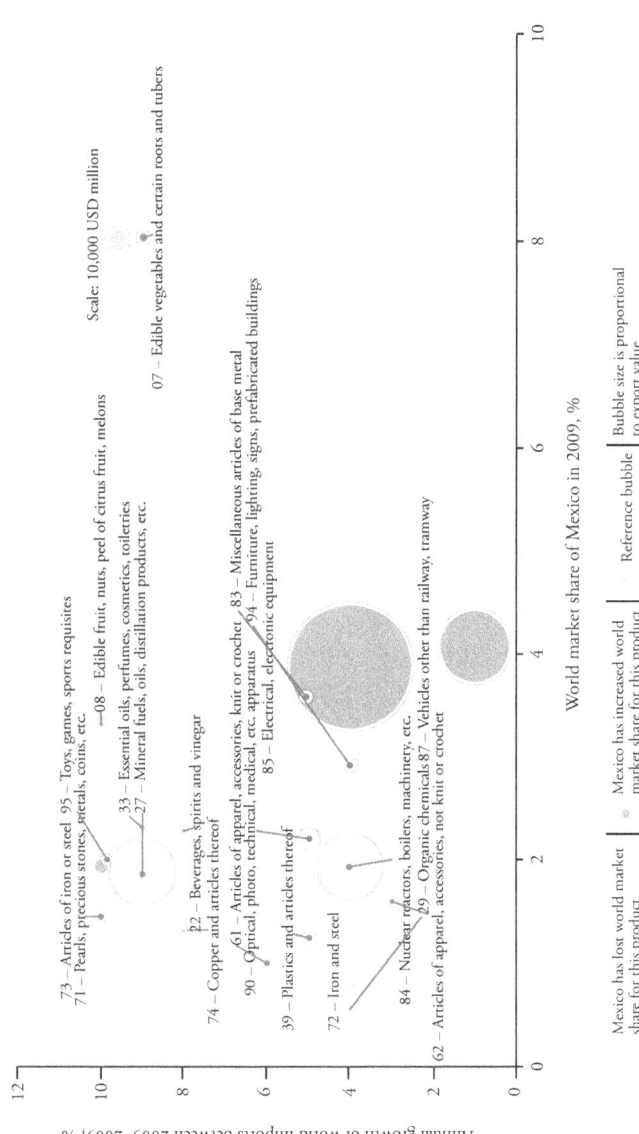

Figure C2.1. Size of national supply and growth of international demand for export products of Mexico (2009).

Source: International Trade Centre, http://www.trademap.org

On the other hand, products such as electrical supplies, electronic equipment, and vehicles other than railway have increased their world market share. This is illustrated by the size of the bubble. One reason for this increase could be that many American companies have established factories in Mexico to assemble electronic equipment that will later on be exported to other countries. This growth in market share can be sometimes deceptive because the products can be considered as reexports or as a trading activity between factories and headquarters in two different countries with an already existing free trade agreement (e.g., Mexico and the United States). Regarding vehicles, it is well known that the presence of important American, Japanese, and German companies in Mexico has helped boost this industry. The main reason is that the Japanese and German companies have seen Mexico as an important gateway to the American market. These assumptions can be easily clarified by performing further research (bilateral trade performance, competitors, FDI, etc.) on the industry/sector, once it is identified.

Growth Strategy: Inclusion of SMEs to the Exports Activities

SMEs are an important source of jobs that generate 72% of national employment and contribute to 52% of GDP. The development of SMEs in Mexico is uneven, as companies are as follows:

1. In development phase—companies that have just begun their exporting activities
2. In the consolidation phase—companies with export experience that are consolidating their production processes and adjusting their operation to the international markets
3. In the diversification phase—companies that are already exporting and require new target markets to grow

For their successful incorporation in global markets, SMEs require comprehensive support schemes. This sector needs to be provided with information, technical assistance, and specialized consulting, as well as support, to increase the business productivity. SMEs in all three phases need to be informed about the requirements they need to fulfill in terms of rules of origin, tariff and nontariff regulations, technical standards, logistics, packaging, and marketing channels, among others, to be able to compete in the international marketplace.

In response to these demands, the Ministry of Economy has created the National Program for the Promotion and Consolidation of SMEs. This program was conceived as a strategy for the inclusion and positioning of Mexican exports in the international market.

Use of Internet Technology to Promote Existing and Mature Markets

The Directory of Mexican Agricultural Exporters arises from a joint project of the National Agricultural Council and the Ministry of Agriculture (SAGARPA) to adopt new strategies for communication, diversification, and positioning of Mexican agricultural exports. Mature sectors such as agriculture require virtual opportunities to do business without intermediaries that will allow them to have a global presence. This directory was designed as an electronic instrument for consultation, where producers and international buyers can identify high-quality food products through a flow of data that is constantly updated and verified. This virtual meeting point translates into real business deals, making it easier for buyers to find information and for Mexican producers to benefit from international promotion that is free and effective.

Design of a Distinctive Image for Mexican Agricultural Products

MexBest is the corporate image that was created by SAGARPA to present and promote Mexican food products that have export quality in the major agricultural and sea products exhibitions around the world. Within this same image, the government decided to create a national brand called "Mexico Supreme Quality" that will differentiate Mexican products from the other international suppliers. Mexico Supreme Quality Brand is an official seal that ensures the safety and superior quality of Mexican products—mainly the ones coming from the agricultural and seafood sectors. The brand, in addition to being a guarantee of quality, aims at the identification and differentiation of products that comply with Mexican standards and international standards in a reliable and transparent way to benefit producers, buyers, distributors, and consumers.

Boosting Growth in Emerging Sectors

The National Development Plan 2007–2012 will also foster opportunities for the development of emerging sectors such as aerospace, automotive, electronics, information technology, chemicals, and renewable energy, among others.

Exports Growth Through Market Portfolio Diversification

To date, Mexico has 12 free trade agreements with 42 countries of Latin America, North America, Europe, and Asia. In the past decade, Asia has become one of the most dynamic and promising markets for Mexican exports. Due to this reason, the Mexican government is launching a strategy to use the Asia-Pacific Economic Cooperation (APEC) forum to develop new governmental and business agreements with the countries of the Pacific Rim and strengthen ties with China, Japan, India, Korea, Australia, New Zealand, and Singapore. The purpose of this strategy is to improve Mexico's relations with these emerging economies of global growth. Through its membership of the Pacific Rim group, Mexico will benefit from the current economic growth, competitiveness, and knowledge emanating from the Asia-Pacific region.

The same strategy will be applied to strengthen the ties with emerging Latin American nations such as Chile and Brazil. Figure C2.2 shows the countries with whom Mexico carries out important trading activities.

As can be seen, the main trading partner is the United States, with a little more than 80% of all Mexican exports. However, as addressed in the National Development Plan 2007–2012, it is imperative that Mexico diversifies its trade portfolio in order to reach more markets and decrease its dependency on the United States. Such information will help the trade promotion agencies and the ministries to design a tailor-made strategy to diversify the target markets.

Therefore, countries represented by darker bubbles, especially the ones in the left upper corner of the graph, represent attractive markets for Mexico. This is mainly due to Mexican exports to these countries have

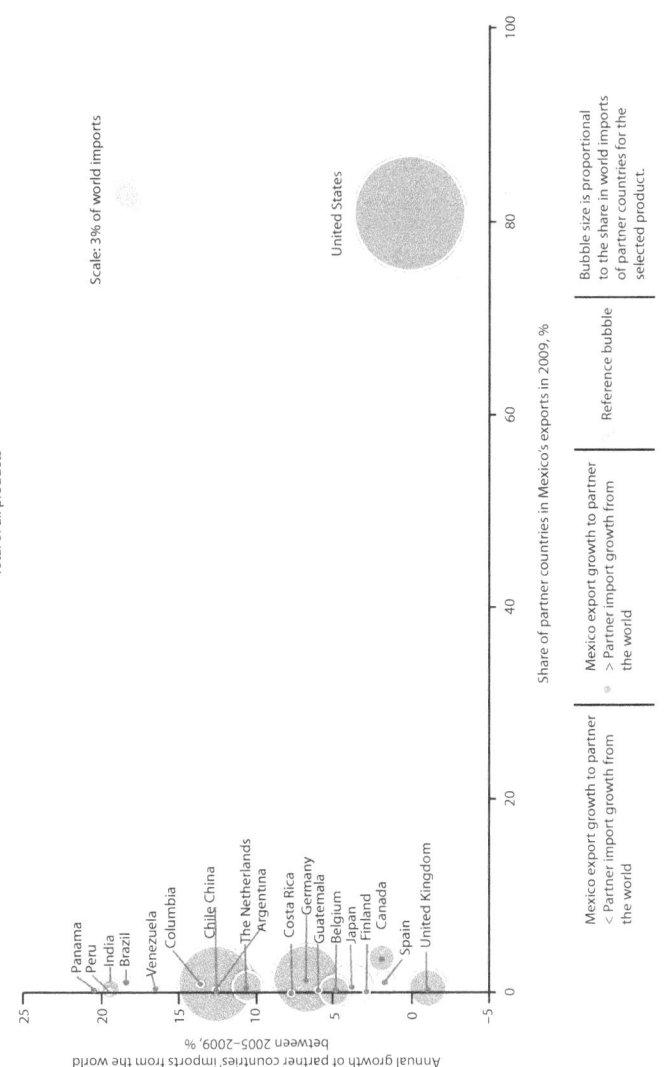

Figure C2.2. Prospects for market diversification for a product exported by Mexico (2009).

Source: International Trade Centre, http://www.trademap.org

grown more than the partner import growth from the rest of the world. This simple analysis shows important data since it can be observed that countries like Panama, Peru, India, and Brazil are importing more and more from Mexico. A more detailed analysis showing which products are imported by which countries is needed. However, this first graph can indicate which markets are priority markets when looking for new potential markets.

Foreign Direct Investment Attraction to Consolidate Mexican Products in the International Market

FDI is an integrated element of an effective economic system and an important catalyst for SMEs' internationalization. FDI triggers technology spillovers, contributes to human capital formation, and fosters international trade integration. FDI in Mexico has opened a wide spectrum of opportunities in the trading of goods and services both in terms of import and export production. Products of superior quality are manufactured by various industries due to the greater amount of FDI inflows in the country.

During 2007 and 2008, Mexico ranked 19th in the FDI Confidence Index.[2] However, due to recent political and economic problems such as the H1N1 outbreaks in the country, the high level of insecurity, and the strong dependency on the American economy, Mexico ranked 24th in 2009.

In response to this situation, the National Development Plan 2007–2012 proposes a strategy that aims to assist investment promotion agencies (IPAs) such as Bancomext in pinpointing the sectors that have successfully attracted FDI in the country, as a guide to identify priority sectors for promotion. It also helps IPAs to identify the countries with whom they compete for foreign investment incentives in a targeted sector and the countries investing abroad by sector.

Functional Analysis

The United Kingdom Trade and Investment Board (UKTI) and Client Satisfaction

From 2005 to the present, UKTI has undertaken an ongoing survey on the satisfaction of its clients, gathering regular data. The purpose of this survey is to determine where clients assess the services offered by UKTI and where improvement could be expected.

The system in place consists of undertaking performance measurements and monitoring supports and delivery of benefit to business by providing (as quoted by UKTI):

- Sound understanding of business needs and how UKTI services add value to which types of clients and under what circumstances.
- Sound understanding of service quality strengths and weaknesses and how they affect impact.
- Robust accountability and measurement of value added to clients' business and to the UK economy.
- Effective performance management—strong customer focus, increased professionalism, and staff skill development.[1]

The rationale behind the survey is to ensure an independent following up with clients by undertaking the following (according to UKTI):

- Comprehensive client records: Who received what help, when, where, and how (using CRM [client relationship management] technology and software)
- Complementing information with clients follow-up: Quantitative surveys of both users and non-users are implemented, using Performance and Impact Monitoring Survey (PIMS) designed by UKTI.
- In-depth interviews with clients: Qualitative studies complement the quantitative surveys with in-depth discussions on particular topics (e.g., checking the contribution of export in accelerating business growth).
- Time series data analysis: Tracking clients' performance over time against comparison with groups of nonusers using independent data sources.[2]

The clients' survey interviews are carried out by an independent market-research firm, by telephone, with an average of 4,000 telephone interviews annually. Client anonymity is protected to encourage genuine responses. The interview is structured to ensure client interest and clear thought about business impact. The calls are done through 20-minute telephone interviews selected from a large random sample, representing around 15% of businesses helped. Interviews are undertaken 4–7 months after delivery of support. The interview records clients' views on quality of service, overall satisfaction, and consecutive business impact, both qualitative (e.g., access to new contacts) and financial (additional sales and profit). Furthermore, follow-up calls are performed with clients who had been interviewed the previous year, to record updated views on business impacts and get estimates of actual and expected additional results. Surveys also record detailed information about client profile, business objectives, development, and export strategy. CRM software is used to make sure that the respondent is the right person in the company.

Clients are asked to rate specific aspects of service quality: Has the quality and relevance of the information or advice provided overall satisfaction? Were expectations met or not? How clearly was information presented? Clients are asked about their overseas business and strategy and previous export experience. Questions are asked about the qualitative benefits to the client's business (e.g., improved overseas marketing strategy; gained access to contacts; if new orders and increased sales have been registered; financial benefit, or additional profit, gained; and, in summing up, improved business performance).

Key Findings and Measured Impact

The quantitative impact was recorded: A total of 15,000 businesses have been helped, and £2.5 billion in additional profit has been generated in the last 3 years; 23,600 businesses clients have been helped and £5 billion in additional profit has been recorded, of which over £35 billion was additional exports. The average additional profit attributed to such support has been estimated to bring between around £100,000 and £200,000 over 5 years of registered records, representing an estimated average additional sales of £700,000–£1,400,000 per client.

Qualitative impact has also been recorded: Clients who report additional sales and profit also report important measurable benefits such as access to contacts not otherwise available and improvements to clients' marketing strategy. High financial impact also reflects accelerated business growth. The largest impacts result when the trade support provided helps clients successfully enter new markets, driving an accelerated business growth. The clients consistently quote the most important aspects of specific support:

- Overcoming barriers to new overseas business
- Gaining access to customers/business partners not otherwise available
- Gaining access to information not otherwise available
- Improving profile or credibility overseas
- Improving knowledge of the competitive environment
- Improving overseas marketing strategy
- Gaining the confidence to explore or expand in an overseas market or markets.[3]

User and nonuser survey results show that clients consistently report greater benefits from exporting by the following:

- Achieving a level of growth not otherwise possible
- Raising profile and credibility
- Gaining exposure to new ideas
- Reducing their dependence on a single or small number of markets
- Utilizing existing capacity more fully
- Increasing the commercial life span of products and services[4]

Trade services also stimulate research and development (R&D), estimated by a separate academic study to average £65k per UKTI client, due to the following factors:

- Exposure to new ideas, new customers, new competitors
- Increased knowledge of competitive environment
- Increased returns to investment in R&D
- New product development due to increased export sales
- Increased revenues providing additional resources for investment in R&D
- Innovative and growing clients most likely to increase R&D as a result of trade support[5]

UKTI by now has collected 5 years of data, allowing strong quantitative analysis on how impact varies by client profile. This shows that firms of all sizes benefit from overcoming barriers to new markets (e.g., gaining access to contacts and networks not otherwise available, raising company profile and credibility in a new market, overcoming legal or regulatory issues). Innovative small and medium-sized enterprises (SMEs) benefit the most from improved marketing strategy, modified products, and changed behavior to upgrade their approach.

However, high financial impact is difficult to predict; no consistent market or profile characteristic predicts incidence of high benefits. Even if innovative SMEs are the main beneficiaries of such a scheme, some large clients also report substantial additional sales not achievable without UKTI help.

Client Profile Insights: By Type of Services Offered and Length of Time Clients Have Been Exporting

UKTI provides a rather large range of services to its clients, among others the Passport to Export service, which focuses not only on inexperienced exporters but also more experienced exporters clients through the overseas network.[6]

Figure C3.1 shows, by type of delivered services, how long the clients' experience is by percentage. (The last group column gives the average total.)

Clients' Estimates of Impact

How realistic are clients' estimates of impact? Periodic depth evaluations and econometric impact studies provide strong evidence. Academic studies rely on econometric techniques to analyze time series data which track UKTI trade clients' performance over time against the performance of a "control group" of nonusers with similar profiles. Econometric results suggest the magnitude of this impact. For example, Passport to Export estimated that clients' asset growth was 26% higher; probability of survival is also higher. An estimated average of £65 million additional R&D funding per firm was generated by trade in services, including Passport to Export and the Tradeshow Access Program, but it should be noted that the average cost of support per client is estimated to be around £10,000.

Service Quality

Quality measures are designed to guide performance management: Clients are asked to rate 4 to 6 different aspects of service quality on a 1 to 5 scale, where 1 = very poor and 5 = very good. Detail varies slightly by service (e.g., for the specific overseas market introduction service [OMIS] provided by UKTI Overseas Network). The quality score for each service is the percentage of clients giving average ratings of 4 to 5. Note that UKTI's target is 80%.

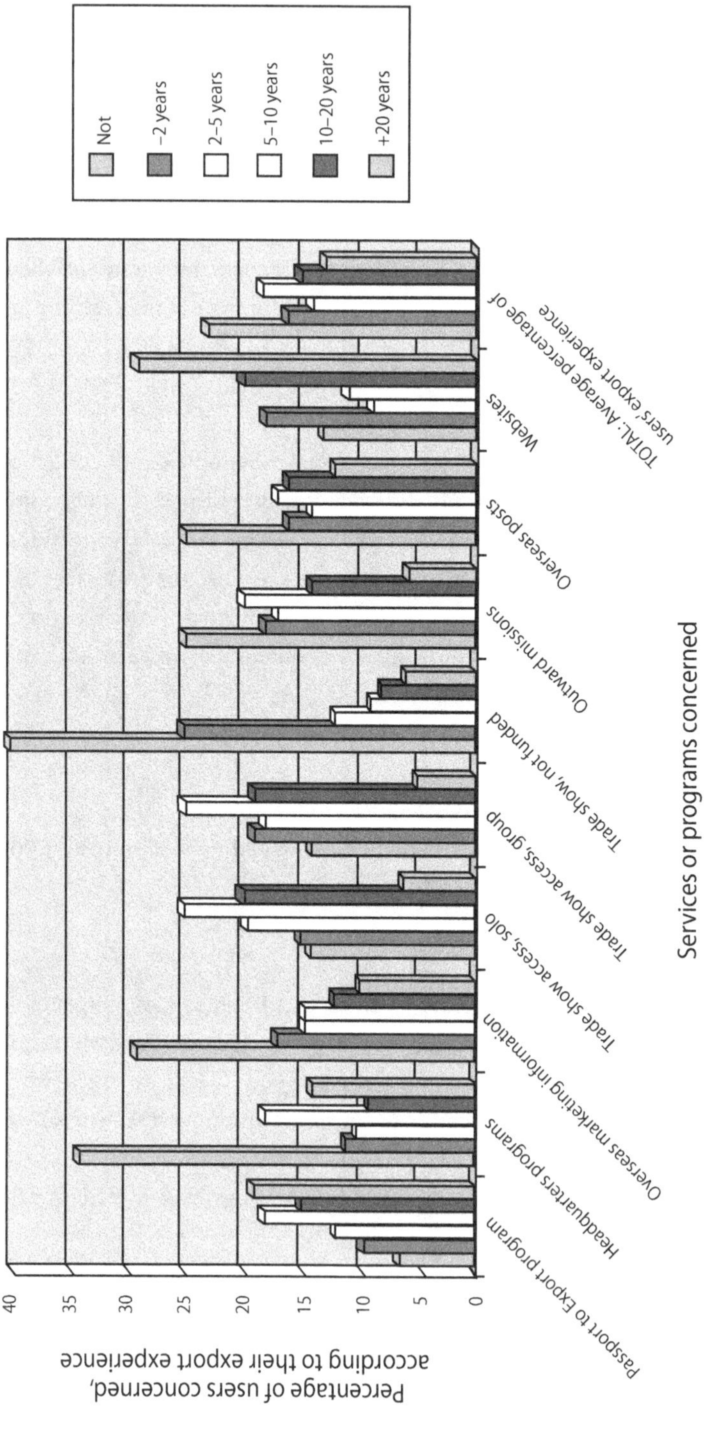

Figure C3.1. Client export experience and programs.

Quality Rating: By Trade Service

Table C3.1 shows that the average quality rating across UKTI trade services is 77%, varying from 53% for the website to 90% for Passport to Export assistance. UKTI has recently upgraded its website to address issues identified by clients.

Table C3.1. Detailed Quality Ratings

Base sample survey	443
% clients giving average scores of 4 or 5 across all questions	**77%**
• Quality and relevance of the information and advice	**70%**
• Clarity and ease of understanding of the information and advice	**85%**
• Quality and relevance of any contacts provided	**63%**
• Communications between your business and the main access point	**81%**
• Communications between your business and the embassy staff (*contact with embassy but not main access point*)	**79%**
• Objectivity and acting in your best interests (*contact with embassy*)	**78%**
• Attitude and professionalism (*contact with embassy*)	**89%**

Fair Trade

Reversing the Trends Through Trademarks, Labeling, and Alternative Channels

Problems Facing the Cotton Sector and the Producers

An estimate of 100 million households are involved in cotton production in 70 countries around the world. The largest cotton producers are the United States, China, India, Uzbekistan, and the west and central African region. Cotton is an especially important source of employment and income within west and central Africa, India, Pakistan, and Central Asia.

Since the early 1980s, the market situation in regard to cotton imports has been changing. They have become less concentrated, and the trend is expected to continue over time. According to the FAO statistics, the number of cotton importing countries rose from 85 in 1980 to 153 in 2009. Moreover, the share of traditional cotton importers has fallen over the past decades. This is the case for the European Union (EU), East Asia, and former Soviet Union countries. Indeed, if these groups shared more than the two-thirds of world cotton imports during the 1980s, their combined import share can be divided by two over the 2000s (33%).[1]

The International Trade in Cotton

Despite increasing local processing (especially in developing countries), cotton is still the main traded agricultural raw material, with more than 30% of cotton production (approximately 6.3 million tons of fiber) traded per annum since the beginning of the 1980s.

It is also interesting to point out that the share of mainland China has been multiplied by almost 6 between the 1980s and 2000s. This increase has been particularly important over the course of recent years and especially since the beginning of the decade 2000. In fact, Chinese imports increased from 52,000 tons in 2000–2001 to 2.5 million tons over the 2007–2008 crop season. This increase may continue in the years to come according to the International Cotton Advisory Committee forecasts, reaching more than 3.8 million tons over the 2012–2013 crop year (about 46% of world imports—again less than 1% in 2000–2001). In 2005–2006, China was the top importer of cotton. Turkey remained the second largest importer for the fourth consecutive season with 8% of world imports (50% from United States, with the rest mainly shared between Greece and Syria).[2]

The world price for cotton has been in steady decline for the past couple of decades. In the 2001–2002 season, cotton prices fell to US$0.92 per kilo—the lowest level in 30 years. While the current price has recovered somewhat, the value of cotton is still only a third of what it was in the early 1980s. The declining value of cotton is a result of the growing use of synthetic fibers like polyester and nylon. Cotton has fallen from 88% of total fiber use in the 1940s to just 40% today. The highly subsidized cotton industry in the United States, the European Union, China, and other producing countries adds further pressure on prices. Cotton producers in the United States receive approximately US$4.2 billion in government subsidies. This is equivalent to the value of their entire crop. About three quarters of the U.S. cotton crop is thus "dumped" on the world market, often priced below the costs of production.

Cotton production in developing countries is less resource intensive and costs less. For example, it costs only US$0.30 to produce a pound of cotton in Benin versus US$0.68 in the United States. Nevertheless, it is the cotton farmers in the Southern Hemisphere who suffer the most from the low global cotton prices, since they rarely receive subsidies.

To reverse the trend, Max Havelaar, one of the main fair trade associations, launched the first fair trade label for a nonfood commodity (cotton) in March 2005. To develop this new marketing approach, Max Havelaar worked with small producers from Cameroon, Mali, and Senegal (about 20,000) organized in association and certified by an international standard organization: Fairtrade Labelling Organizations International (FLO). Cotton growers from Burkina Faso also joined this enterprise by the end of 2005, and cotton farmers from this country are likely to account for the greatest share of the global fair trade cotton production.

In order to implement this new fair trade segment, Max Have-laar entered into partnerships with the French company DAGRIS and benefited from the financial support of several sources (e.g., the French Ministry of Foreign Affairs and the Centre for the Development of Enterprise). Fair trade cotton products are sold off by using different brand names (e.g., Armor Lux, Célio, Cora/influx, Eider, Hacot, Colombier, Hydra, Kindy, La Redoute et TDV industries).

The purpose was to benefit from a better market price for cotton seeds. An increase of 46% compared to the price paid for the traditional cotton seeds originating from Senegal and 26% compared to the price paid for the traditional cotton seeds originating from Mali was observed over the period of 2004–2005, which even reached 60% for the 2005–2006 campaign.

Benefits of Fair Trade for Cotton Producers

Since the introduction of the first fair trade minimum prices for cotton in 2004, fair trade has demonstrated that it can substantially improve the lives of cotton producers. By selling to the fair trade market, cotton farmers have the security that they will receive a minimum price that aims to cover their average costs of sustainable production. They also receive a fair trade premium that allows them to invest in community projects, such as schools, roads, or health care facilities.

To benefit from such market price differential, a label was created and producers were certified under this label. The benefit was then redistributed to certified producers. To obtain certification, the producers had to meet particular specifications (e.g., use cotton-made bags rather than polypropylene ones and ensure a better sorting of the cotton seeds). Moreover, the textile fabrics were also certified as "fair trade cotton." It should be noted that production costs were audited to check whether the International Labour Organization (ILO) conventions were respected. The price granted for fair trade cotton seeds follows the scale given in Figure C4.1.

Conclusions drawn in Mali after 2 years of fair trade cotton presence were positive. Indeed, in some regions in Mali, the extra income enabled farmers to buy new agricultural material, cattle, and furniture for schools; enroll children in school; and pay teachers' wages. It was then decided to renew and enlarge the scheme, given its encouraging results.

Figure C4.1. Cotton prices under fair trade regulations.

Source: InfoComm, http://unctad.org/infocomm/anglais/cotton/market.htm#fair

Fair Trade Standards for Cotton

Among other things, fair trade standards in cotton ensure the following:

- The fair trade minimum prices for cotton are set at different levels depending on the producing region. The minimum prices always cover the costs of sustainable production. Furthermore, if the market price is higher than the fair trade minimum price, the market price applies.

- Fair trade minimum prices for organic cotton are set 20% higher than the fair trade conventional minimum prices.
- In addition to the fair trade price, buyers must pay a fair trade premium of US$0.05 per kilo of fair trade seed cotton. This is used by the producer organizations for social and economic investments such as education and health services, processing equipment, and loans to members.
- Environmental standards restrict the use of agrochemicals and encourage sustainability.
- Pre-export lines of credit are given to the producer organizations if requested, of up to 60 % of the purchase price.

Fair Trade Certified Cotton Producers

Fair trade cotton producers are usually small family farms organized in cooperatives or associations that the farmers own and govern democratically. The only exception is in India and Pakistan, where some cotton-producing communities are not organized in cooperatives but are selling to a commodity board. This board is responsible for transferring to the individual farmers the extra benefits generated by fair trade sales.

Since the 2004–2005 period, the trend has completely changed. Table C4.1 shows the fair trade cotton sales in volume for 2008–2009. Such a growth rate for 2008–2009 seemed exceptional but were confirmed in 2010–2011.

It is worth noting that the whole cotton market has changed drastically in 2011: Cotton has been recorded as the fastest commodity price increase in 2011, over and above corn, coffee, silver, heating and crude oil, and even gasoline. In fact, the Reuters/Jefferies Commodities Performance Index [JCPI]), a global commodity benchmark tracking 19 commodities (that are mostly U.S. traded), is at the highest level since

Table C4.1. Fair Trade Cotton Sales in Volume (2008–2009)

	Conventional	Organic	Total	Growth rate
Cotton (as used in 1,000 distinct items)	25,280	2,292	27,572	94%

its launching in 2004 for cotton. The average change in cotton price in 2011 was up by 35%, with a 52-week high of US$219.70 and a 52-week low of US$72.96.

Cotton producers who are part of fair trade organizations will benefit from such prices, but all other producers, who are dependent on the traders' practices and intermediaries, will unfortunately not necessarily benefit from this evolution.

Enlarging the Experience

Fair trade is not only involved in the cotton trade; it has reached other sectors using the "fair trade" label as a trade promotion tool. It became also clear that a regional approach was needed, to approach more local producers.

As of 2009, there are 827 producer organizations in 60 countries; an 11% increase over 2008. It should be noted that membership is voluntary and many small producers are not yet part of a network. Fair trade standards cover 20 product groups as the number of consumer products made from fair trade certified goods continues to grow. Cocoa and sugar saw strong leaps in sales thanks in part to 100% commitments by global chocolate and confectionary brands including Cadbury, Dairy Milk, Nestlé, Ben & Jerry's, and Green & Black's. Coffee, the pioneering fair trade product, also experienced steady growth.[3]

Table C4.2. Fair Trade Producers Around the World: Members in 2010

Regions/Numbers	Africa and the Middle East	Asia	Latin America and the Carribean
Number of Producers Countries	28	12	20
Producers Organizations	231	120	476
Members and workers	760,000	189,000	280,000

Award-Winning Fair Trade Products

Fair trade products are gaining recognition not only for ethical leadership but for excellence in taste and quality—thanks to producers' superior fair trade ingredients crafted by partner businesses into award-winning products. FLO calculates the total estimated retail-sales value based on both out-of-home sales and retail sales, since this more accurately reflects what consumers spend on fair trade products. Out-of-home sales come from products consumed outside of the home (e.g., in restaurants and coffee shops). Retail sales come from consumer products bought in stores and supermarkets.

In 2009, the following countries calculated the out-of-home sales value using the average out-of-home retail price (e.g., the average price of a cup of coffee at a café): Canada, Finland, Germany, Ireland, Spain, and the United States.

Out-of-home retail price often has a higher value per volume sold than the retail sale price found on products in stores. Therefore, the countries that use the out-of-home retail prices for their calculation may have higher growth rates. Out-of-home sales make up approximately 19% of the total global estimated retail sales. The estimated retail value of fair trade certified products is reproduced in Figure C4.2 (unfortunately on 2004–2007 statistics, but the trend has been confirmed since then).

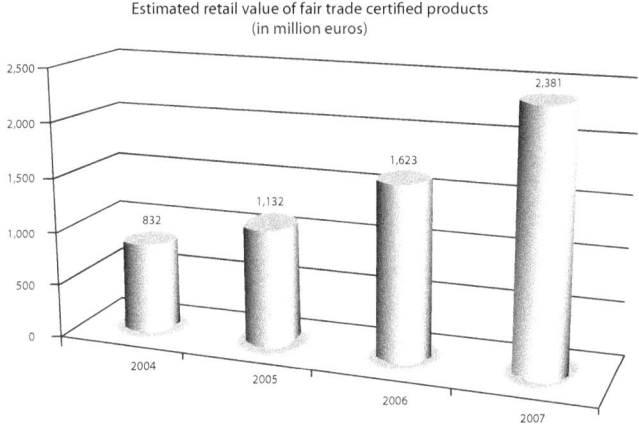

Figure C4.2. Estimated retail value of fair trade–certified products.

Source: http://www.fairtrade.net

Results Achieved in 2011

Fair trade standards now cover 20 product groups as the number of consumer products made from fair trade certified goods continues to grow. Such recorded trends—despite volatile market fluctuations and competition among suppliers and distributors—show that the concept has gained growing recognition, not only at consumer level but also in the traditional supply and distribution channels. It can definitely be considered as a valuable alternative tool for nontraditional trade promotion strategy, beyond its own ethics values.

Conclusion

Strong trade promotion organizations (TPOs; using labeling and certification) in the commodity sector can be developed and expand their role to reversing trends or at least minimizing the impact of commodity price fluctuations on producers by creating and developing alternative trade channels. This also implies a kind of solidarity between producers and consumers through international branding and labeling, even by accepting to pay a premium if necessary. It seems that this idea is more and more adopted and accepted by consumers, challenging the traditional distribution channels.[4]

Useful Link

Fairtrade International (http://www.fairtrade.net)

PART III

National Trade Promotion Cases

CASE 5

Australia

The Australian Trade Promotion Environment

Building Awareness for Export

Australia's export promotion efforts are conditioned partly by the fact that the country has only about 25,000 exporters, just 4% of all businesses. This compares with 15% in Canada and much higher proportions for European countries and export-oriented countries like Mauritius. Most exports are handled by very large enterprises, and Australia is far away from its principal trading partners.

In April 2002, the commonwealth, state, and territory governments agreed on a goal of doubling the number of exporters by 2006. The federal government supported this commitment with budgetary measures, increasing the number of regional TradeStart offices (an export-readiness training program) by 50% and doubling the minimum grant available under the country's principal export promotion cofunding scheme. This effort was aimed at new exporters, especially small and medium-sized enterprises (SMEs). Following these new measures, the goals have been achieved despite the 2008–2009 economic recession, which did not affect Australia with the same impact as in the developed countries.

Applying a Cofinancing Policy for Trade Promotion

Australia's export promotion system is unique among the countries analyzed in that it distinguishes between two types of services: free and fee based. The rationale that drives the effort is that the principal justification for government assistance is to correct the information asymmetry between SMEs and larger firms. Therefore services that help "intenders" and "new exporters" build export readiness, select target markets, and obtain initial market information are free. Customized services that help companies understand and enter new export markets are charged on a full cost-recovery basis.

Financial assistance is provided through export-market development grants (EMDGs), a cofunding system that is structured to integrate a wide range of costs. This eliminates the need to integrate subsidies into specialized programs, such as trade missions and trade shows. In 2001–2002, about US$98 million was distributed to 3,078 companies, an average of about US$32,000 per company. Funding for this program has been regularly increased over the years.

Austrade: The National Trade Promotion Agency

The Australian Trade Commission (Austrade; http://www.austrade.gov.au) is the federal agency responsible for promoting Australian exports and international business. Austrade's specific mandate is to reduce the time, cost, and risk associated with selecting, entering, and developing foreign markets. Austrade is managed by a board of directors that is accountable to Parliament through the Department of Foreign Affairs and Trade (DFAT), and its overseas offices are located in Australian embassies and consulates around the world.

Resources

Austrade has more than 1,000 employees, just over 500 of which are assigned to 94 offices in 60 countries. In addition to direct delivery of services through 15 national offices, it funds 2 regional programs delivered in partnership with private and public organizations across the country. Austrade's operating revenue in 2002 was US$148 million, of which US$21.5 million was derived from sales to clients, with the balance coming from the government. Additional funding of more than US$100 million was allocated to the EMDG program, which operates under its own legislation. Another US$15 million over 4 years has been provided for a training program delivered by regional partner agencies. Not all these resources are allocated to trade promotion, since Austrade also promotes foreign direct investment (FDI) and provides consular services in some locations.

Organization

The Austrade Board of Directors has 12 members with representation from both business and government. The government is represented by the secretaries of the Department of Foreign Affairs and Trade and the Department of Industry, Tourism, and Resources.

A semi-independent agency, Austrade has a recruiting program that stresses business knowledge. Most export promotion staff are recruited from the private sector and have advanced degrees and experience in either consulting or specific industries. Austrade's compensation scheme offers performance bonuses.

The Australian Operations Division focuses on exporter development, international business services, and trade promotion. Trade promotion includes providing assistance to Australian exporters to participate in foreign trade shows and arranging appointments with visiting trade commissioners. Market research and intelligence and provision of in-market support to Australian exporters are mainly the responsibility of overseas offices. There is, however, an industry specialist group in Australia that focuses on globally oriented industries like tourism and environmental products and services. Regional trade commissioners throughout Australia provide local support.

Resources are allocated to overseas markets with the best sales prospects for Australian products. Because some priority sector markets do not have embassies or consulates, Austrade provides consular services at its offices. The offices are located strategically in the country to focus on key sectors that are buyers for Australian exports. The number of staff allocated to each region, however, does mirror the size of the trade relationship. Trade professionals in foreign offices are a mixture of Australians and locally hired sector experts.

Objectives and Priorities

Austrade's services, including market research and intelligence, are funded on a fee-for-service basis. Export-readiness and export-preparation programs are provided through private and public partner agencies. Priorities, therefore, are largely established though consultations with these partners. Many of the partner organizations operate regionally. For example, regional partners, including state governments and private organizations, deliver TradeStart, an export-readiness training program.

Resources Research

Austrade's market research activities are spread throughout the organization. The agency therefore uses a wide variety of databases and other Internet resources that vary from country to country. Austrade officials say they use the U.S. Department of Commerce reports and a variety of free trade–related sites, as well as subscription-based databases, including the Gale Group and Marketplace company databases. They maintain a list of useful published sites, partly by subscribing to *Really Useful Sites for International Trade Professionals*, published by the Federation of International Trade Associations (FITA; http://www.fita.org). FITA maintains an online index of more than 7,000 international trade web resources, including subscription databases.

Other Government Agencies Involved in Trade Promotion

Austrade is also active in the government-wide Market Development Group, which coordinates all federal government trade-related activities. It maintains a relationship with AusIndustry, a business-support agency in the Department of Industry, Tourism, and Resources, which promotes FDI in Australia. Austrade also collaborates with state and territory governments, each of which has an economic-development entity that provides some export promotion assistance, focused mainly on SMEs. Regional programs include the New South Wales Export Adviser Program, the Queensland Mentoring for Growth Program, the South Australia Export Assistance Program, the Tasmania Export Marketing Assistance Scheme, and the Victoria First Step Exporter and Going Global Programs.

Trade Promotion Initiatives and Actions

Tools for Raising Awareness

Austrade is promoting public awareness of the benefits of overseas trade and building a positive international image for Australia. Its most important awareness-raising program is *Exporting for the Future*. Its educational component is delivered through secondary schools as training and learning resources for teachers. Austrade's booklet, *Helping Take Your Business to the World*, is used for first-time exporters to raise the awareness of Australia's export services and to promote the Austrade brand. The monthly newsletter, *Export Update*, is also available on the website and contains news of upcoming trade events, success stories, and information about services available to exporters. In association with the Australian Chamber of Commerce, Austrade administers the Australian Export Awards. The agency also maintains an Export Awards Hall of Fame.

Tools for Building Export-Readiness

Austrade has two linked export-readiness programs, TradeStart and Export Access. Companies that become export ready can begin market-entry activities under the guidance of export counselors. This includes counseling through the process of visiting the target market (at company expense) and follow up.

TradeStart/Export Access is delivered by local offices, at regional level, with a program that provides training to SMEs and links to Austrade's global network. It is also developed and delivered by regional partners, through more than 30 TradeStart offices as well as outreach agencies.

The "Are you ready to export?" section of Austrade's website provides an export-readiness checklist as well as information on capabilities that a company must develop before beginning to export. This checklist consists of a detailed assessment questionnaire, the "Export Capability Tool," filled in by the exporting company. The exporting company then receives an online automated assessment of their export capability and the opportunity to be contacted by an Austrade export counselor.

Selecting Target Markets

Market information and advice is provided to Australian enterprises through 15 Austrade offices and more than 30 TradeStart offices. First-time exporters receive a set of free information about the general market conditions and economic dynamics for individual markets. A wide variety of country guides and sector market reports are also available from the Austrade website, providing an introduction either to a country market or to a global sector.

Cost of Participation

When firms consider themselves ready to enter into foreign markets, they are provided with detailed research, industry analysis and business-matching services as well as market entry assistance. "Tailored solutions" can be obtained for a fee of about US$130 per hour. First-time customers get a lower rate for the first 10 hours. Initial consultations are free and when customized work becomes necessary, Austrade officials begin providing clients with cost quotations. These fees are eligible for cofunding under the EMDG program. Companies can also register for free trade briefing reports provided by the Economic Analytical Unit of the Department of Foreign Affairs and Trade.

Cofinancing through export market development grants provides assistance for SME export development activities in general, with exporters selecting the specific components they need. (Note that this approach is similar to Canada's.)

The EMDG program provides grants of up to 50% of eligible export promotion expenditures over a threshold of AU$15,000 (about US$10,400). The minimum grant is about US$3,500. A company can receive eight grants plus three more for each new foreign market entered, but the grant can be reduced under an export performance test that is applied starting with the third grant. This is a reimbursement program, and companies do not need to be preapproved. They apply for the grant at the end of their fiscal year for money spent during the year. Any company with income of less than AU$50 million (US$35 million) can apply, provided that its products have at least 50% Australian content or meet certain other criteria.

The program allocates export promotion expenses into seven categories:

1. Export market representatives and consultants
2. Marketing visits
3. Overseas buyer visits to Australia
4. Communications
5. Free samples
6. Trade shows, seminars, and in-market promotions
7. Promotional literature and advertising

A few categories have spending limits (mainly the daily subsistence limited to US$150 a day and no first-class air fares), but companies are free to allocate the resources as they see fit.

Since funding is capped and expenses are not preapproved, expenses are reimbursed using a "split-payment" system. Companies entitled to a grant of more than AU$60,000 (US$41,500) receive that amount as an initial payment upon submission of an application at the end of its fiscal year. Once all participating companies have received their initial payment, the size of the second payment is calculated on the basis of remaining funds available.

For reimbursements, Austrade uses a sophisticated risk-profiling model that results in on-site audits in nearly 60% of cases, but more than 80% of claims are paid out within 8 weeks. Most grants go to individual companies, but some are allocated to industry associations and joint ventures formed by groups of SMEs. On average, 60% of grants are given to companies employing 20 people or fewer, and only 10% of claims come from large companies of more than 100 employees.

Austrade uses direct mail promotion aimed at business associations to promote the program, and it keeps in touch with previous recipients who do not renew assistance after their first claim to record their reasons for not continuing the assistance program. Australia is using EMDGs as its principal export promotion assistance scheme. It increased funding and lowered eligibility thresholds in 2002.

Matching Opportunities

Another component of Austrade services designed to connect exporters with foreign buyers is an online directory of exporters on its website. Users can search by product or they can access overviews of key Australian sectors. The agency uses a single website for foreign buyers and local exporters. There is also a database of market opportunities. There is no formal matching service, but trade commissioners provide matching on an ad hoc basis.

Trade Shows

Austrade does not provide financial assistance for participation in trade missions, trade shows, or incoming buyers missions, but does offer trade show services for a fee. It maintains a short list of best exhibitions around the world, and it stages country pavilions at key trade shows. Services include consulting to assist the exporter in selecting an appropriate exhibition, understanding in-market business practices, preparing an exhibit, and arranging follow-up appointments. These services are eligible for cofunding under the EMDG program. Promotional activities for Australian industries can be cofinanced through the EMDG program, industry associations, or joint ventures between concerned companies in a particular sector.

Closing Export Deals

Because overseas staff are trade commissioners and part of diplomatic missions, they may not act as company marketing representatives. They will, however, provide a wide range of support services, customized for the needs of individual customers. These services include introductions to qualified buyers, market intelligence, and assistance with product launches. They are eligible for cofunding under the EMDG program.

Assessment of Export Promotion Practices

Austrade uses the most systematic performance-assessment techniques of any of the trade promotion organizations (TPOs) studied. Each of the agency's three trade-related "outcomes" (awareness raising, export services, and export finance assistance) is subdivided and assigned a target with results being measured annually. Some measures are related to the volume of activity, while others are purely results oriented and based on survey data. For example, under *awareness raising*, the number of events is counted, the number of positive media is mentioned, and the proportion of survey respondents indicating "unprompted awareness of Austrade" is calculated, along with broader measures of community awareness. Similarly, export services are rated according to both the volume of activities and their export impact, in terms of the number of clients and the dollar revenue volume. Export impacts are also systematically assessed on a sector-by-sector basis, and all of this information is used to improve export promotion efforts.

Evaluating the Effectiveness of All Programs Components

As a whole, Austrade considers that linking export-readiness training with individual coaching for first-time exporters is the most effective component of the domestic program. The export market selection advice, which is integrated into the training programs under the TradeStart/Export Access module, is considered extremely valuable.

The strategy of preparing new exporters through free services and then linking them to customized fee-based services, starting with an initial 10-hour partially subsidized consultation, has proven very effective because it creates a bridge from general export and information services to company-specific market entry strategies.

Austrade considers that the reason for TradeStart/Export Access success for first-time exporters is based on carefully selected target markets. The value of this service consistently shows up in satisfaction surveys as a "greatly appreciated" service by clients.

The EMDG program is regarded as very successful, both in performance and cost-effectiveness. Annually, on average, Austrade approves grants for more than 3,000 companies, totaling US$100 million, with an average grant of about US$32,000. Given the threshold of more than US$10,000 and a cofinancing factor of 50%, this implies average spending on export promotion by these companies of about US$75,000. The value of exports generated by recipients is estimated at more than US$5 billion, creating an estimated 60,000 jobs. The client satisfaction rates 88%. Client satisfaction is assessed through the "Performance Measurement Annual Client Survey," including satisfaction ratings and measurements of the export impacts of Austrade services.

Registering with the Austrade exporter database and accessing the related opportunities database provides an extremely cost-effective way for Australian companies to establish a permanent presence in their target markets, alerting them of opportunities that may come up.

Conclusion

Austrade opportunity matching systems that provide export promotion officials with information about exporter capabilities are seen as critical to the success of other program elements, even though they may not generate immediate sales on their own.

Such a multidimensional/interrelated approach proves to be efficient, both for Austrade as a resource provider and its clients, even if the impact may not be immediately measured. There is a lesson to draw on the necessary continuity of links and programs over the years between the trade promotion institutions and the companies: It is necessary to follow them from the first steps in the export business till they become confirmed/experienced exporters.

CASE 6

Canada

An Integrated and Decentralized Range of Trade Promotion Services and Tools

Major Features of the Canadian Foreign Trade

The foreign trade structure in Canada is characterized by unusual patterns. First, the close links between the U.S. and Canadian economies and the continental economic integration resulting from the North American Free Trade Agreement (NAFTA) is illustrated by trade statistics: More than 80% of Canada's exports are for the U.S. market. Most trade represents the amount of intercompany transfers and flows between multinational enterprises, which counts for an average of US$1.5 billion per day. Second, the distribution of trade flows is illustrated by a rather narrow distribution: 4% of exporters are responsible of 85% of the total value of transactions. Third, small and medium-sized enterprises (SMEs) exporting less than US$1 million per year total 40,000, which represents the bulk of the exporter's population. For these reasons, Canadian trade promotion efforts are targeting SMEs.

Sharing the Export Costs: An Innovative Approach

As in many other countries, the main obstacles to SME exports are a lack of export know-how within firms, inadequate foreign market information, and poor capacity to manage risks on foreign markets. Therefore, Canada is making special efforts to provide trade information, specialized training, counseling on foreign trade access, and in-market assistance. Most of these services are provided free of charge. Only a few subsidies are provided for specific trade promotion activities initiated by individual companies. Financial subsidies for direct promotion are the exception. But in order to support medium- to long-term trade expansion strategies, a cofinancing scheme for general export development in individual companies is refundable, based on exporting success. However, a non-repayable grant program helps export associations in priority sectors.

Team Canada: The Focal Point of Trade Promotion

Canada does not have a single export promotion agency but rather a "virtual trade agency" called *Team Canada* (http://www.canadabusiness.ca). The Department of Foreign Affairs and International Trade (DFAIT) is the lead department for Team Canada.

The Team Canada concept was introduced in 1995 to coordinate the export promotion efforts of all government departments in Canada, with DFAIT as its lead department. Within this structure, DFAIT's Trade Commissioner Service (TCS) takes on a specialized role, identifying and assessing emerging markets, improving Canadian access to those markets, and providing market intelligence and support. Under the business model developed to meet these challenges, the market research center takes on market information responsibilities, preparing country guides and market profiles. (In the past this work had been handled previously by local consultants at foreign posts.) Under this structure, trade commissioners spend more time outside the office, building networks of contacts and gathering market intelligence.

Team Canada Objectives and Priorities

Team Canada's officials say that they do not formally target particular markets, except when they may be influenced by Industry Canada's export strategies. For the most part, resources are allocated to sectors and products where clients are active and where officials in each country develop a periodic trade action plan based on client needs.

Officials note that as a result, the effort is not proportionate to export volumes. Many of Canada's exports are commodities for which trade promotion has only a minor role, and a substantial proportion is predetermined by intercorporate transfers by multinational enterprises. As a result, services are mostly taken up by SMEs, and their requests drive the allocation of resources.

At the sectoral level, Trade Team Canada Sectors (TTCSs) establish trade promotion priorities. Each group is made up of federal and provincial government experts and representatives of sector associations and companies. About half of all TTCS members are from the private sector. Each team has designated first-tier and second-tier priority markets. Each has a private sector co-chair and benefits from the participation of DFAIT posts in priority markets.

Tools for Raising Export Awareness

Numerous resources are provided for companies interested in becoming exporters. The most important is *Roadmap to Exporting*, a 24-page booklet that provides a complete set of export promotion services. DFAIT's free newsletter, *CanadExport*, is published twice a month, both in print and in electronic formats (http://www.publications.gc.ca/pub?id=258016&sl=0). The newsletter contains selected exporting success stories, current and upcoming trade events, and information about the use of export assistance resources.

In order to raise awareness of exporting as a profitable business activity, DFAIT organizes the annual Canada Export Awards (http://www.exportawards.ca/exportawards), companies can apply or be nominated. At the annual trade conference of the Canadian Manufacturers and Exporters, 25 finalists are chosen and winners are selected in 12 categories to receive awards. Winners benefit from media coverage, and their profiles are distributed to Canadian trade missions around the world. Winners can use the Canada Export Awards logo in their promotional material for 3 years.

Spreading the Resources

DFAIT's budget on plans and priorities includes about US$200 million for international business development. Support for Industry Canada and Team Canada is drawn from a wide base budget and staff resource, including full-time and part-time staff allocations, with no formal budget. Industry Canada estimates that about US$28 million was allocated for implementing export promotion strategic programs in 2006–2007. (Contributions made by the other federal departments have not been published.)

When Team Canada was created, Industry Canada already had an extensive network of business service centers throughout the country, which has been maintained. The Canadian province and territories have 13 centers and 380 regional access partners. These centers provide a wide range of support services, including some export assistance. They are operated jointly between the two departments, with DFAIT providing seconded trade commissioners to staff offices in Industry Canada's facilities. These centers are the principal instrument for delivering all types of assistance, focused largely on SMEs.

Within Team Canada, Industry Canada was also charged with organizing export promotion at sector level. TTCSs are in charge of this. These trade teams build partnerships between the federal and provincial governments, together with exporting companies and industry associations. At the moment 13 sector groups are now active; two are led by Agriculture and Agri-Food Canada and the Department of Canadian Heritage. Industry Canada and the other departments organize trade missions for these sectors jointly with DFAIT, conducted by the federal and provincial ministers in charge of each sector.

Internet Access

Most of Team Canada's services are accessible over the Internet, operated as a *virtual network system*. Canada has the second-highest cable television penetration in the world, so low-cost broadband Internet connectivity is available to virtually every potential exporter, making the use of advanced web techniques fully operational. The website for the province of Manitoba[1] provides a single interface for all information assets throughout the nationwide system.

The Trade Commissioner Service (TCS)

DFAIT's TCS is the key source of export promotion expertise because many of Industry Canada's trade services are provided with seconded DFAIT staff. About 500 trade commissioners are posted at headquarters in Ottawa and elsewhere in Canada, while 135 of Canada's 164 missions are posted in 114 countries. This approach is unusual among the countries studied because it does not concentrate resources in sector hubs. For example, the Canadian TCS has staff in nearly every country in Africa, while Austrade (for Australia) is present only in South Africa.

The TCS recruits trade commissioners through public competitions. Most recruited commissioners are new university graduates, fluent in French and English, as well as other languages, with degrees in commerce, economics, or international trade. They receive extensive training as part of a foreign-service career. Where the size of foreign missions permit, commissioners are assigned sectors, but because they rotate regularly through domestic and foreign assignments, they tend not to acquire sector expertise, as is expected in some other agencies. Locally engaged staff provide sector contacts in larger missions.

Trade commissioners at foreign posts are informed of sectoral developments in Canada by returning to Canada two or three times each year and participating in DFAIT's outreach program. They network with exporters in their assigned sectors and participate in trade events. They also have access to the international business opportunity center, an internal resource operated by DFAIT and Industry Canada. The center provides trade commissioners with sector expertise and assists with opportunity matching.

Trade commissioners and other trade professionals assigned to departmental headquarters are organized into area "desks" that oversee foreign trade promotion efforts in assigned regions and to international trade centers across Canada. The market research center in Ottawa creates country/sector profiles, gathering information from a wide range of online databases and hiring consultants in target countries. Foreign posts do not conduct market research, but they review all reports for accuracy before they are published.

The Virtual Trade Commissioner

The Virtual Trade Commissioner (VTC) was launched in November 2002. Registered Canadian companies are provided with a personal password-protected VTC web page that contains market information and business leads. The web pages are continuously updated with personalized market information, including market reports, business news, events, and business leads matching the user's product or industry. To register, a company must be Canadian-owned or be a foreign subsidiary of a Canadian company, and it must offer products or services with at least 50% Canadian content. The company must also register with the Canadian Capabilities Database because this is a two-way system that links Canadian companies with trade commissioners around the world. The VTC is a free service. The VTC allows users to do the following:

- Build a personalized web page that contains country information and business opportunities reflecting the company international business interests.
- Access current market reports, sector-specific news, and trade events.
- Receive assistance and request services from trade commissioners located in Canada and target markets.
- Be notified when new information is published.
- Manage online applications to existing funding programs, such as Investment Cooperation Program (INC), Invest Canada-Community Initiatives (ICCI), and Global Opportunities for Associations (GOA)—all of these programs support businesses, communities and associations.

The VTC online exercise consists of seven steps:

1. Setting up the page
2. Searching international markets
3. Accessing business contacts
4. Expanding international business
5. Using extra tools
6. Getting the latest information directly delivered
7. Meeting with the trade expert.

The VTC process also consists of seven phases:

1. Visitors fill out their account and create their profile. Information is needed on their sectors and countries of interest.
2. The client can then look for a target market, selecting a country, accessing countries of interest, or expanding to more countries. At

this stage, a VTC can give assistance to help clients make the right decision

3. When needed, clients can ask for help from various Canadian organizations who are ready to assist. Additional market information can be provided for finding qualified foreign contacts, potential buyers, partners, agents, technology sources, special advices on market access, and so on.

4. Clients can access country information such as profiles, import regulations, economic overviews, and so on. When prepared to enter into business, they can find business offers and procurement opportunities.

5. On the left side of the client's page, extra information is constantly updated about credit conditions, including their credit profile; insurance, including an online insurance service (with free quotes offers); procurement; customers; and conditions for getting financed, selling to governments, and so on.

6. Clients are notified when information is updated by setting their own preferences (daily, weekly, monthly, which day of the week/month, etc.).

7. At that point, clients may leave the VTC for an appointment with a real trade expert.

In case of need, a 34-page guide is available.[2]

The VTC is also promoting Global Value Chains (GVC). GVC is a new business model that helps global competitiveness, profitability, and long-term sustainability. More information is available through *Linking in to Global Value Chains: A Guide for Small and Medium-Sized Enterprises.* GVC provides various business strategies. The GVC reports also investigate multinational enterprises, their procurement needs and methods, as well as the business opportunities they might offer to Canadian firms.[3]

The VTC network offers market reports that are also available by industry sector and by region/country.[4] VTC market reports provide a detailed analysis of industry sectors that enables businesses to take advantage of opportunities abroad. Over 600 reports are available free of charge. (Of course, this market/country information relates to sectors of interest for Canada and are available to any subscriber.)

It should be noted that such services are on a common platform jointly developed by Agriculture and Agri-Food Canada, Foreign Affairs

and International Trade Canada, and the TCS. These federal departments all contribute to sector expertise and in some cases run their own
export assistance programs. The most important of these are the Agri-
Food Trade Service operated by Agriculture and Agri-Food Canada;
the Canada Mortgage and Housing Corporation (CHMC); and Trade
Routes, operated by the Trade Department of Canada.

Building Export Readiness

The concept of export readiness drives the design, planning, and operations of Team Canada. Companies that are not ready to export are
directed to Industry Canada's national network of business service centers and international trade centers, where they can access a full range of
export-readiness resources.

Team Canada, through Industry Canada, offers numerous self-
assessment tools and self-help handbooks. Key resources include *Export
Diagnostic*, an interactive online self-assessment tool.[5] Registered users
can create a series of export scenarios as they develop an export plan. *Take
a World View* (http://publications.gc.ca/pub?id=50555&sl=0) is a similar
tool for the service sector. A self-help guide, *Step-by-Step Guide to Exporting*, is also available online and in print. This 60-page booklet covers the
entire process, from identifying opportunities to developing and execut-
ing an export plan. Team Canada also provides an online market-entry
preparation tool, *Interactive Export Planner*,[6] which takes users through
the process of creating an export plan. *Speaking Globally: An Exporter's
Guide to Effective Presentations* is a guide to presenting products and services to foreign customers.[7]

Developing Market Entry Strategies

Two programs help firms develop and implement market entry strategies
for specific markets. DFAIT's ExportUSA program[8] provides seminars in
Canada combined with visits or minitrade missions to the United States.
The program has three versions: introductory seminar, introductory seminar plus visit to a consulate in the United States, or advanced seminar
plus minitrade mission to the United States.

The second program, New Exporters to Overseas (NEXOS), organizes 7-day missions to Europe. These are organized on a regional basis, through Industry Canada's business service centers. At least six companies must participate, and they are encouraged to work through an industry association or chamber of commerce. ExportUSA and NEXOS programs are partly funded by the government, which pays for organizing each program, including speakers, training materials, and logistics. Participating companies pay for their own travel and accommodation.

Specialized Export Training

In addition to workshops and seminars organized by the international trade centers, more specialized training is provided by the Forum for International Trade Training (FITT). This industry-led organization, funded by Human Resources Development Canada, offers skills development on three levels. First, it offers 3-hour *Going Global* workshops online and at locations across Canada. Second, it offers a series of eight courses known as *FITT skills* that are accredited with the International Association of Trade Training Organizations (IATTO). Third, participants who complete all eight courses receive a FITT diploma accredited by IATTO, which entitles graduates to use the Certified International Trade Professional (CITP) designation. The eight courses cover entrepreneurship, marketing, finance, logistics, market entry and distribution, research, law, and trade management.

The classroom version of *FITTskills* is delivered through approximately 35 educational partners across Canada, mainly community colleges. The program is also delivered via a distance-learning system to a limited number of registered participants. FITT also offers individually tailored international trade training for companies, as well as a customized version of *FITTskills* for the service sector.

Selecting Target Markets

Team Canada offers many country guides and country/sector reports, mostly published by DFAIT's market research center in Ottawa (with some of them prepared by private consultants). These are available for download in PDF form through an interface that gives the user the option of country or sector orientation.[9] Users must be Canadians, and they must register.

The market research center uses a wide variety of online resources, including many international information sources, to prepare these reports. They obtain local market information mainly through private consultants. Until several years ago, such reports were contracted to local consultants by the foreign posts. This system was changed as part of the restructuring of the TCS in the late 1990s, which shifted the emphasis of foreign posts to collecting market intelligence and assigned market information functions to headquarters in Ottawa. Country and business guides cover such topics as bidding on government contracts or selling services in selected target markets.

Identifying Sales Opportunities

Program for Export Market Development

Export promotion efforts of individual SMEs and industry associations are cofunded through the Program for Export Market Development (PEMD). This provides broad-based support instead of subsidizing activities. Upon submission of receipts, PEMD reimburses eligible expenses.

Assistance for companies is limited to firms with annual sales between Can$250,000 and Can$10 million (US$190,000 and US$7.5 million, respectively). Assistance is in the form of repayable cofinancing of up to 50% of costs for approved export development activities. Companies that have developed 1-year international marketing plans are eligible for the market development strategies component. They can obtain funding for market visits, incoming buyers missions, participating in trade fairs, product testing for market certification, legal fees, transportation costs for offshore trainees, and various other costs. The annual contribution from PEMD is a minimum of about US$3,800 and a maximum of US$38,000. The contribution is repayable based on 4% of incremental sales in the target market over 4 years.

Companies with little exporting experience are eligible for the new-to-exporting component of PEMD. They can obtain assistance to develop an international marketing strategy. The maximum contribution is about

US$5,700 and can be used for either a market identification visit or participation in an international trade fair. The contribution is repayable based on 4% of export sales in the target market over 2 years.

The PEMD capital-budgets-bidding component is aimed at manufacturing, engineering, construction, architecture, and management-consulting firms. Companies competing in international tenders for major capital projects worth more than about US$750,000 are eligible. They can obtain between about US$3,800 and US$38,000 in 50% cofunding annually to pay for the preparation of bids or proposals. The contribution is repayable in full if there is "contractual success" in the target market within 3 years.

PEMD also provides assistance to trade associations on a cost-shared basis. This reflects the government's policy that public subsidies should promote sectors rather than individual companies. To qualify, trade associations must represent their sector on a national basis, and the proposed activities must involve generic export promotion, improved market access, or the provision of market information and intelligence. Contributions are nonrepayable based on a flexible formula and an assessment of the proposed activities. Annual contributions are between US$15,000 and US$75,000.

Trade Missions

Team Canada supports market entry through a multilayer program of trade missions. At the highest level, Team Canada trade missions are led by the prime minister and the minister of international trade, with participation from provincial premiers. These are national efforts designed to develop country-to-country business relationships. They present multisector export offers in three or four of the most important markets in a region. Companies are invited to participate based on their potential for new business development and their activity in one of several business sectors that are featured on a mission. Canadian trade missions follow the same model but are led by the minister of international trade and are focused on individual sectors. These missions are organized by the TTCSs and require strong commitments from exporters.

The government has an explicit policy that its role is facilitation, not leadership or physical staging, of trade missions. It expects industry associations to organize business support for outgoing missions. Logistical services are contracted to private companies in the target market, and the fees are divided among participating companies. The government pays for the costs of its own participants.

Trade Shows

TCS officials consider trade shows effective export promotion tools only for companies that are well prepared. They encourage sectoral trade associations to coordinate the efforts of multiple companies in their sectors.

The Team Canada Brand Canada program, operated by DFAIT and Industry Canada, is almost entirely associated with trade shows. Team Canada provides the hardware for country pavilions at sector trade shows, but companies or industry associations cover the costs. These expenses are eligible for cofunding under the PEMD program. There is no national brand advertising, although some sector groups fund small advertising programs in advance of trade shows, usually through trade publications. Foreign posts in some countries also conduct limited country brand advertising when they find that Canada's image is poorly perceived. Canada faces a unique problem compared with the other countries studied in that its integration with the United States makes it difficult to project a distinct image abroad. This view reflects the fact that Canada faces a serious identity problem in many markets. Foreign buyers and industry associations interviewed by DFAIT consultants have consistently revealed that they are unaware that certain products in their markets are Canadian. This is especially so for high-technology products, which they perceive to be of U.S. origin.

Finalizing Export Sales

TCS offers six core in-market services:

- Market information
- Key contacts
- Visit information
- Local company information
- Face-to-face briefings
- Market access and advice

This assistance is provided to Canadian exporters subject to specific guidelines. A principal rule is that a trade commissioner must offer only services that he or she is prepared to provide to any Canadian company that asks for it, regardless of company size. Trade commissioners may not act as a marketing representatives for Canadian companies. They will make appointments but will not otherwise act for the Canadian company except to ensure that international treaties are respected. Trade commissioners make introductions and will accompany company representatives to meetings, but they will not act on their behalf when they are not present. Team Canada does not provide direct technical assistance for product standard compliance in target markets. It refers companies to the Standards Council of Canada, which assists Canadian companies in having their products accredited abroad. While companies are expected to pay for accreditation services directly, cofinancing is available under the PEMD program.

Matching Trade Opportunities

Canada's international trade-opportunity matching system is based on three separate databases:

1. The Canadian Company Capabilities Database maintained by Industry Canada is a database covering more than 50,000 businesses.
2. DFAIT's World Information Network for Exports (WIN Exports database is focused on experienced companies).
3. DFAIT also offers a free automated opportunity-matching service through international business opportunities centers based on company profiles provided during registration. Foreign buyers can access information about Canadian capabilities from the "Doing Business With Canada" (DBC) cluster, which is part of the "Non-Canadians Gateway" on Canada's main website.[10] Buying from Canada is one of five elements of the DBC cluster, which also includes "Investing in Canada," "Establishing a Business in Canada," "Selling to Canada," and "Partnering in Science and Technology." A key goal of this cluster is to refer foreign buyers and investors to Canadian trade commissioners in their home countries.

Trade commissioners at foreign posts and exporters use these databases on an ad hoc basis and in response to requests from the VTC service.

Conclusion: An Assessment of Export Promotion Practices in Canada

Team Canada evaluates program effectiveness almost entirely on the basis of client satisfaction, as measured through systematic annual surveys. The most recent survey indicated a near 80% approval rating. Although client surveys involving free services tend to be positively biased, Canada's export promotion programs are considered successful by current and former officials, as well as by private-sector users. The main criticism from the private sector is that like the government itself, the export promotion program tends to be managed by self-evaluation rather than by rigorous internal assessment. The TCS conducts a client survey every 2 years, and in the intervening years it conducts an employee survey. On the basis of these assessments, export promotion programs have been restructured a number of times.

Trade commissioners consider that business intelligence is their most important product provided outside Canada. They say that trade fairs are successful only when they have a strong sector focus and build the image of Canada as a source of world-class products and services in that sector.

Financial assistance to individual companies for market entry works for some companies but does not have a consistent track record, especially in weaker sectors. For this reason, Team Canada encourages companies to enter foreign markets in groups.

Private sector exporters confirm that the most valuable services provided are business intelligence and contacts.

One of the conclusions of the client survey was that while clients like the emphasis on intelligence and contacts, they perceived that the quality of intelligence was not as good as it could be. In response, the TCS carried out another effort, known as the *New Approach@Work* (NA@W). This initiative is renewing focus on value-added services and more effective use of electronic tools to deliver information to both staff and clients. The initiative also encompasses a series of training and professional development modules to be disseminated worldwide. These modules cover subjects such as proactive market intelligence gathering, investment, excellence criteria, sectoral training, risk analysis, and international financing. The TCS is also acting to ensure that the department's intranet is used more effectively to disseminate information on best practices for trade commissioners. The intranet will also be used more intensively to provide trade commissioners with access to virtual learning materials, e-bulletins, an e-newsletter, information on sources of financing, science and technology partnerships, and the International Business Opportunities Center (IBOC) services.[11]

Conclusion

All of these online services provided by the Canadian institutions for trade promotion are rather extensive and obviously at the forefront of information technology. Furthermore, most are interrelated between different trade promotion actors and can be used on a complementary basis, by home as well as by foreign agents. This makes the whole Canadian tools and services offered online for trade promotion tools quite impressive.

Mauritius

A Success Story

The Overall Perspective

Mauritius is an economic development success story. Success has been due largely to the effective planning and management of a series of national export strategies. Over the past 35 years, these strategies have moved Mauritius from a high-unemployment, single-crop economy (sugar) to one that is characterized by nearly full employment, a significant manufacturing sector, and an internationally oriented service sector.

The export success of Mauritius has been largely a consequence of foreign direct investment (FDI) attracted by the country's political and social stability, its abundant and educated workforce, and its preferential access to the European Union (EU) and U.S. markets for sugar and textile exports. This strategy is completed by a strong export promotion program designed by Enterprise Mauritius (EM), established as a public-private institution in partnership with the chamber of commerce, industry associations, ministries, and public institutions.

What is the Specific Mauritius Approach?

The current export strategy reflects the lessons learned and the results of decisions taken over the past years. However, Mauritius's circumstances are nevertheless changing, and Mauritius planners have learned from experience that an export strategy must be flexible and updated constantly.

The Mauritius export strategy follows 6 goals and the "3 Cs" approach, as defined by EM:

- *Competitiveness enhancement* focuses on diffusing technology, developing enterprises, providing working capital, and sourcing clean energy.
- *Product conformity* provides support for upgrading product quality, standards, and packaging.
- Market connectivity involves surveys of markets with export potential, business meetings, international trade fairs, and financial assistance to companies exploring foreign markets.

The 6 goals formulated for the Mauritius strategy settings are outlined in the following sections.

Goal 1: Support the Development of the Enterprise

The country's first attempt to initiate economic diversification came in the early 1960s. An integrated strategy was introduced to favor import-substitution manufacturing and attract foreign investment. The basic principles for the strategy formulation process were as follows:

- Infrastructural-, institutional-, and enterprise-development programs were launched in parallel.
- The Bank of Mauritius was established to provide long-term credit facilities.
- An economic planning unit was created to monitor economic development strategic implementation.
- The University of Mauritius was founded to facilitate industrial development.
- Fiscal incentives were introduced to attract potential investors, particularly in import substitution industries.
- Tax legislation was progressively revised to stimulate enterprise development.

The impact of this initial strategy was, however, more limited than expected. Unemployment at the beginning of the 1970s remained high (29%), economic growth was low (1.75% per year on average), and manufacturing accounted for a mere 6.4% of the gross domestic product (GDP). The country had also a chronic trade deficit. What was wrong?

In the early 1970s, Mauritius introduced a mixed import-substitution export development strategy, which was maintained throughout the decade. Priority continued to be placed on facilitating private enterprise development. An export processing zone (EPZ) was established, efforts to attract FDI were initiated, and a wide range of incentives was provided to firms engaged in the domestic market ("certificate enterprises"). The banking sector was encouraged to provide easy access to short- and long-term financing.

These measures had a strong impact on Mauritius's growth rate: The economy has grown at an annual average rate of 20.6%, and by the 1980s, employment in the manufacturing sector had nearly quadrupled and the unemployment rate was cut in half in one decade, according to the World Bank Data and Statistics. Of equal importance were the indirect, intangible effects of the strategy's focus on enterprise development. The import substitution aspect of the strategy, in particular, produced entrepreneurs with skills and industrial experience. It exposed the labor force to a new working environment and an "industrial culture."[1]

Goal 2: Anticipate Shifting Circumstances and Competitive Advantages

Throughout the 1980s, it became increasingly clear that the impact of the mixed economic development strategy could not be sustained. While the import-substitution strategy generated a spirit of enterprise, the highly effective rate of protection—tariffs, quotas, and exchange controls—did not allow local entrepreneurs to be sufficiently exposed to market pressures to develop managerial skills and the other expertise needed to compete internationally. It was solely in the protected sectors that higher profits, wages, and employment were being achieved.

During this period, two devaluations in 1979 and 1981 had not been sufficient to offset a growing balance-of-payment problem and general stagnation of the manufacturing sector. From the early 1980s to the 1990s, increasing emphasis was then placed on sustaining the momentum of the export-led component of the mixed economic development strategy.

Export incentives were introduced and reinforced. Numerous import restrictions were eliminated and the tariff system was reformed. The Mauritius Export Development and Investment Authority (MEDIA) was created to strengthen export and investment promotion. This was reinforced by the creation and development of Entreprise Mauritius (EM), a trade promotion organization (TPO) with joint partnership between the public and private sectors.

A proactive, overseas market development–support program was launched, targeting niche opportunities for garments in the EU and U.S. markets. Promotion in the regional Common Market for Eastern and Southern Africa (COMESA) also became a focus of EM's attention.

Priority was assigned to the further development of the EPZ and, in particular, its value-added contribution to national production. Foreign investment in the garment sector was, and is still, actively promoted.

This export-led strategy enabled Mauritius to follow the international trade growth since the early 1990s. The economy benefited from favorable terms of trade, falling prices for imported oil, cheaper imports (due to the depreciating U.S. dollar), and political uncertainties prevailing in countries with high capital-export potential.

It should be mentioned that the rate of unemployment has remained so low that Mauritius has a shortage of manpower, which is quite unique within the region. Such a situation encouraged prospective investors to look to Mauritius as a base for taking advantage of preferential terms of access with the European Union and the United States.

As a result of this strategy, the following has occurred in Mauritius since the 1990s:

- The number of enterprises operating in the EPZ increased five times to more than 550.
- Employment in the EPZ increased four times to 90,000.
- Net exports increased 18 times.
- The EPZ's share of national value-added increased from 18% to 48%.

With full employment, however, Mauritius lost its labor-based competitive advantage, both in terms of costs and ability to generate or absorb new labor-intensive production capacities. A second competitive advantage—that of preferential market access in the European Union—is also being eroded with the elimination of quotas under the World Trade Organization (WTO) agreement on textile and clothing.

In response, the government has again shifted its strategy. The aim now is to put Mauritius in the upper-middle income group of countries through a modified national export strategy. This strategy involves a shift from the production sectors into the goods and services sectors, which are not handicapped by limited space, volume requirements, or distance.

The new strategy focuses on obtaining greater efficiencies in traditional foreign-exchange earning industries, like sugar, textiles, and tourism. It also focuses on developing the export earning capacities of the following sectors: manufacturing; nonsugar agriculture; and regional financial, commercial, and maritime services. A flexible approach is also adopted for import of foreign labor, to overcome the obstacle of shortage of manpower. Finally, new priority has been placed on regional cooperation.

Goal 3: Build an Institutional Base That Supports and Facilitates Competitiveness

A major importance is attached to the maintenance of an institutional infrastructure that directly promotes, supports, and facilitates broad-based private sector involvement in the international marketplace (as opposed to controls). An institutional structure has gradually been developed on the principles of institutional specialization and interinstitutional coordination.

The governmental bodies, beyond the EPZ already mentioned, which are directly or indirectly involved in international trade promotion are the following:

1. *Business Freeport Services Ltd.(BFSL).* In November 2001, the Business Park of Mauritius Ltd. (BPML) incorporated a subsidiary company, BPML Freeport Services, Ltd. (BFSL), to develop and provide logistics and ancillary telecommunications facilities and services to operators trading under the Freeport, EPZ, for Suspended Duty/Bonded regimes and local enterprises.

2. *Entreprise Mauritius (EM).* EM is a collaborative partnership between industry and government that aims to help businesses in Mauritius expand into regional and international markets and develop their internal capability to meet the challenges of international competition.

3. *Board of Investment (BOI).* With the aim to attract international investment in the country, the BOI is the national investment promotion agency falling under the aegis of the Ministry of Finance.

4. *Financial Services Promotion Agency (FSPA).* The FSPA was set up on December 1, 2001, by parliament under the Financial Services Development Act. The agency is a body corporate administered and managed by a board and funded by the government to facilitate access to export credits and services offered to foreign investments.

5. *Industrial and Vocational Training Board (IVTB).* The IVTB is a parastatal organization operating presently under the aegis of the Ministry of Training, Skills Development, Employment, and Productivity to set up and organize vocational training programs for business operators.

6. *Mauritius Freeport Authority (MFA).* MFA's mission is to promote and encourage Freeport trade, including transit and merchandise trade, and to position Mauritius as a logistics, marketing, and distribution hub in the region.

7. *Mauritius Standards Bureau (MSB).* The MSB was established as a division of the Ministry of Commerce and Industry by the Standards Act of 1975 to set up, control, and diffuse standards for national products. The main objective is transforming "Made in Mauritius" into a mark of excellence. To promote this quality image, MSB provides a certification-making scheme for products and processes (MAURICERT) and operates a National Quality System Certification Scheme for the registration of firms to ISO 9000

8. *State Investment Corporation (SIC).* The SIC is the investment arm of the Republic of Mauritius for stating and controlling the investment policies at national level.

9. *The Export Processing Zone Development Authority (EPZDA).* The EPZDA, established in 1992, acts as facilitator and catalyst of Mauritius' export competitive edge. It provides free-of-charge consultancy services to identify and assess management and technical problems.

10. *The Small Enterprises and Handicraft Development Authority (SEHDA).* The SEHDA was created to rationalize and optimize the use of resources dedicated to the small-business sector.

From all these institutions, the most important one for export promotion is EM, a TPO resulting from a collaborative partnership between the Mauritian public and private sectors.

EM sought to reinvent itself from a trade support institution and TPO to a comprehensive trade development organization. It did so in developing "the 3 Cs model," which focuses on competitiveness enhancement, product conformity, and *market connectivity*. EM tested and used the 3 Cs model in three specific areas:

1. *New market development for small and medium-sized enterprises (SMEs) in the Swedish market.* This project supported Mauritian SME clothing manufacturers in developing export opportunities in Sweden. Between 2006–2009, exports of clothing to Sweden grew from less than 2 million rupees to nearly 10 million rupees.
2. *Demystifying the U.S. market for SMEs.* This project sought to help Mauritian agroprocessing and textile companies enter the U.S. market. Between 2008–2009, exports by large enterprises increased 21%, while SMEs without prior U.S. export experience realized 69% growth.
3. *Creating an action plan to inform and prepare SMEs to meet new EU product regulations.* In 2008, not a single Mauritian SME was exporting to the EU. By June 2009, three SMEs were regularly exporting processed food to France with a value of nearly 5 million rupees. The 2010 results confirmed the trend in expanding the scheme to other sectors.

Every year, EM coordinates the participation of businesses in various domestic and international events such as trade fairs, buyer–seller meetings, B2B (business-to-business) meetings, contact-promotion programs, and conferences. EM also facilitates joint ventures and inward buying missions. Other EM activities include the following:

- Country briefs and market intelligence reports
- Assistance in the development of new products for existing markets or for new markets
- Assistance in conducting market tests of sample products with potential buyers

- Dealing with issues relating to trade barriers (e.g., nontariff barriers and technical barriers to trade)
- Provision of a web-based marketing and e-commerce transaction platform and access to offshore resources for conducting market research

EM won the World TPO Award 2010 for the "Best TPO from a Small Country." The award was presented at the 2010 biennial TPO Network World Conference and Awards, hosted by ProMexico—the national trade promotion body of Mexico—in conjunction with the International Trade Centre (ITC). This event brought together more than 150 participants from 50 countries to address the theme "Building Export Success—Enhancing TPO Impact in a Changing Global Environment."

ITC, in delivering this award, pointed out that as a small island developing state, Mauritius took an integrated approach to its clients, addressing both their needs and the needs of the market.

Goal 4: Emphasize Institutional Linkages, Government-Business-Labor Partnerships, and Networking

Special attention is given to developing and implementing national export strategies on a partnership basis among government, business, and labor organizations. For example, public- and private-sector representatives are on the board of all specialized national organizations involved in trade promotion. The chairpersons come from the private sector.

The government also meets twice a year with the Joint Economic Council (JEC). The JEC's mission is to promote free enterprise and the interests of the Mauritian private sector. JEC members include the Mauritius Chamber of Commerce and Industry, the Mauritius Chamber of Agriculture, the Mauritius Employer's Federation, the Mauritius Export Processing Zone Association (MEPZA), and all other major business associations in the country. JEC forms part of the national negotiating team for the EU trade agreements, the Sugar Protocol, and all regional and multilateral trade agreements.

Goal 5: Promote Regional Collaboration, Capitalize
Geographic Positioning, Create Specialized Services, and
Increase the Role of Mauritius as a Financial Hub

The previous strategies of Mauritius had been designed to take full advantage of commercial opportunities generated by preferential trade agreements (in previous years, the Lomé Convention, General System of Preferences [GSP], and the Sugar Protocol). Focus was accordingly directed toward the European and American markets. While these traditional markets continue to be significant, the success of the country's current strategy is also based on the development of the regional markets and active participation in regional trade agreements. The region comprises 350 million consumers and imports the equivalent of US$25 billion annually.

Mauritius Freeport Authority (MFA) aims to motivate business operators to use the geographical position of Mauritius as a regional distribution hub. The Freeport Initiative is in keeping with the diversification strategy deemed necessary in the post–General Agreement on Tariff and Trade (GATT) era. In 1992, Mauritius launched the Freeport Authority. The advantages the Mauritian economy could derive from the Freeport activity include the following:

1. Generating more trade between Mauritius and neighboring countries
2. Attracting foreign businesses
3. Generating employment in export and services
4. Encouraging the upgrading of port facilities

Freeport activity has developed rapidly since its creation. Freeport imports are mainly from China, Thailand, India, and South Africa, while exports are primarily toward Madagascar, South Africa, and Reunion Island. Exports are mainly in textiles, electrical appliances, and chemical products.

To reinforce its commercial involvement in this regional market, Mauritius has established its Freeport as a duty-free zone for all goods destined for reexport. For operators, all machinery, equipment, and materials can be imported duty free into the Freeport. The legislation provides for a comprehensive package of incentives for companies looking for a cost-effective storage, assembly, and redistribution location.

The incentives set in place include the following:

- A zero-rate tax on corporate profits and free repatriation of profits
- Exemption of tax on dividends
- Reduced port-handling charges for all goods destined for reexport
- Access to offshore banking facilities
- Possibility of selling a percentage of total turnover on the local market

As a result of such policy, the amount of reexport of the Freeport zone has been multiplied by 10 since 1995 (from US$18 million). Beyond the active promotion of the EPZ and Freeport, Mauritius' strategy calls for SMEs located outside the zone to engage increasingly in exporting.

Human resource development is given particular attention under this aspect of the Mauritius export strategy. All its trade support institutions are now engaged in training and skills development in one form or another. One example can be given with training for operating bilingual call centers (French and English) with abilities in Chinese, due to the cultural origins of the local population.

The government places a 1% levy on the aggregate payroll of all enterprises operating in Mauritius. This sum is remitted to the IVBT, established in 1989 with the following mandate:

- Promotion of employee training through fiscal and financial incentives
- Setting up training facilities while ensuring that there is no duplication
- Enabling private training institutions to respond effectively to human resource development needs while ensuring improvement in the quality of the training provided

Goal 6: Promote the Development of Specialized Export Services

Besides manufacturing, the service sector is growing in importance and contributes to the country's success. As early as 1981, the Export Service Zone Act was introduced to stimulate the reexport of manufactured goods. This was to be achieved by setting up firms to engage in merchandizing trade and to provide specialized export marketing and related services to the domestic manufacturing sector. Incentives were extended to such firms.

As a consequence of this strategic decision, Mauritius has not only developed an important reexport business but has acquired considerable expertise in translation, marketing, business consultancy, and other exportable services where emphasis is on the use of new information and communication technologies.

Financial Services

The Mauritius government and the private sector have collaborated effectively to create an environment in which the financial services sector is promoted and expected to become a major part of the island's economy. Legislation for offshore banking was introduced in 1991, supplemented by lower tax rates for particular types of banks. From the start, the local regulatory authorities decided to maintain a high level of credibility: Only foreign banks with a recognized international reputation are approved to do business in the country.

Conclusion: The Mauritius Trade Promotion Strategy

Mauritius has benefited from a public-private sector partnership as well as from an active network of trade support institutions focusing on specific sets of services, ranging from capacity building, business facilitation, and research, through offshore market development. With the constant changes taking place on the international arena, each institution constantly addresses the new challenges ahead.

Useful Links

National Computer Board (http://www.gov.mu/portal/sites/ncbnew/main.jsp)

Enterprise Mauritius, "About Enterprise Mauritius" (http://enterprisemauritiusw
.biz/wm/general-about-us/about-enterprise-mauritius.html)

The Mauritius Freeport (http://www.efreeport.com)

WTO case study, Andrew L. Stoler, "Mauritius: Co-operation in an Economy Evolv-
ing for the Future" (http://www.wto.org/english/res_e/booksp_e/casestudies_e/
case26_e.htm)

ITC, "Trade Support Institutions" (http://www.intracen.org/wedf/images/ef2001/
cpmauritius2.htm)

Taiwan

Integrating a Multipurpose Infrastructure and Focusing on Trading Services

Taiwan's Trade Promotion Program and Institutions

The National Institutions for Trade Promotion

The Taipei World Trade Center (TWTC), which started in 1986, is an integrated site promoting foreign trade. Jointly sponsored by the government and industrial (as well as commercial) associations, it assists domestic businesses and manufacturers in reinforcing their international competitiveness and coping with the challenges they face in the foreign markets. In addition, TWTC undertakes many initiatives to help foreign businesses establish a wider presence in the local market.

The TWTC offers an impressive and complete platform for the international business community: Their integrated business complex combines exhibition space, conference facilities, offices, and hotel accommodations for international business, in a space that includes an exhibition hall, International Convention Center, International Trade Building, and Grand Hyatt hotel. In fact, this infrastructure is part of the World Trade Center (WTC) network. It also has the ambition to serve as a model for global trade centers.

Besides TWTC, the national authorities have recently built a multipurpose exhibition complex, the Nangang Exhibition Hall.[1] This complex has all sorts of facilities for large meetings, symposia, and international trade shows, whose program is closely integrated with TWTC.

The National Institution for Trade Policy: The Bureau of Foreign Trade

The Bureau of Foreign Trade (BOFT; http://eweb.trade.gov.tw/mp.asp?mp=2) is the focal institution for the following:

- Trade administration (national regulations and commodities)
- Trade relations (multi- and bilateral trade)
- Trade promotion per se (companies, product promotion, and trade shows)
- Statistics and forecasts
- Trade facilitation programs (implementation and expected benefits, but materials should be updated)
- Overseas offices

The trade policy strategic goals are stated every year by the BOFT. For example, in 2009–2010, they were as follows:

1. Strengthen trade facilitation and simplify the documental operation process to achieve the goals of trade management.
2. Participate actively in the World Trade Organization (WTO) and other international trade organizations and improve the Taiwanese international trade environment.
3. Sign foreign trade agreements (FTAs) with important trading partners and adapt to regional and international economic integration.
4. Enhance the image of Taiwanese products and assist exporters to promote their own brands and channels in overseas markets.

Some Findings and Assessment: Visibility and Beyond

The online access to more details on policy goals and on major functions is quite limited and (as of early 2011) does not provide much detailed information. Most queries, specially for recent or forecast information, return blank web pages on the BOFT website. The Taiwan External Trade Development Council (TAITRA), more recently, seems a new, dynamic, and strong-willed partner for foreign business, at least on the Web. The TAITRA website is mostly a databank for outsourcing business.

This does not mean that the Republic of China's trade promotion strategy and programs are not there (as everyone knows the trade success of Taiwan's overseas business). Taiwan's private business initiatives and direct trade contacts are mostly left to the private sector, not so much controlled or led (except on trade fairs and exhibitions), in contrast with its powerful neighbor, China.

Promoting the Service Industries as a National Priority

Taiwan's service industry has been developing rapidly and is becoming an essential component of the industry's current output: it accounts for 68.6% of gross domestic product (GDP) and about US$269 billion in 2009. The trade services promotion tool is operated by TAITRA, which has its own overseas offices. TAITRA has a mandate to develop Taiwan's service industry. To this end, TAITRA started the Service Industry Promotion Center in July 2006, to facilitate the globalization of Taiwan's service industry.

The center is focusing on four service areas, according to the trade promotion service sector national strategy program:

- Information technology
- Medical tourism
- The construction and environmental engineering industry
- The cultural and creative industry

Information Technology

As Taiwan's enterprise software market is expected to maintain 9.2% compound annual growth rate from 2006 to 2012 and reached NT$8 billion in total value by 2010, Taiwan's information service industry's output is growing steadily as well. This is driven mainly by the growth of platform architecture integration; corporate demand for instant decision analysis; Taiwanese manufacturers being spread widely over the Asia-Pacific region; and offshore outsourcing becoming, according to its promoting agents, a mainstream phenomenon.

There were 8,800 Taiwan-based service providers in 2006, mainly in the areas of enterprise software service, information security, digital content, and embedded software. Revenue of the Taiwanese information security industry has been on the rise due to strong export demand. The overall Taiwanese embedded software market topped US$30 million in 2008 and nearly US$40 million in 2010.

For digital content, with the fast growth of Chinese-language content market, Taiwan aims to be the hub for development, design, and manufacture of digital content in the Asia-Pacific region. Such services can also work by adapting other languages for the Chinese-language content.

The Taiwanese information service market and industry are projected to continue expanding in the future. Expenditure on information service is expected to rise in both the Asia-Pacific region and domestically. A large demand for information service will lead to growth for outsourcing, consulting services, and cross-border content development.

For health care, the trade promotion strategy is clearly stated: According to the worldwide health ranking by The Economist Intelligence Unit (EIU), Taiwan ranks second, with health care quality comparable to the United States and Europe but at one-fifth to one-sixth the cost.

Medical Tourism

With an emerging health care phenomenon of traveling outside one's home country to receive quality health care at affordable prices, the international medical services industry is a rapidly growing global market that is presently being aggressively developed by both public and private sector health care organizations, especially in Asia-Pacific areas where the costs of procedures performed at the most advanced health care facilities are a mere fraction of the cost of identical procedures performed in the United States, Japan, Europe, or Middle Eastern countries. Along with the rising awareness of "lifestyles of health and sustainability," individuals are becoming more conscious of their own health and are willing to search globally for better medical services by accessing open information platforms. This innovative sectoral approach will be replicated in other trade promotion service industries.

Construction and Environmental Engineering Industry

Taiwan takes pride in its many construction accomplishments, most notably such recently completed large-scale projects as the Taiwan High-Speed Rail (which is the first in the world to combine the European and Japanese high-speed rail systems), the Hsuehshan Tunnel (which is the world's longest road tunnel consisting of two primary tunnels—one of the most difficult engineering projects ever built), the Taipei 101 Tower (which challenges the world's tallest building), a modern freeway network, and the metro rail system. Owing to the quality construction and design of these projects, Taiwan has won global recognition and is looking to cooperate with foreign countries in the field of infrastructure.

Currently, Taiwan has 12,000 construction companies and 1,000 engineering consulting firms. Various leading construction companies and consulting firms have undertaken overseas projects since the 1960s, mainly in Asia and Middle East region. The projects include harbors, buildings, airports, roads, and industrial and residential development, as well as industrial turnkey projects, which have comprised the majority of recent works. Take Continental Engineering Corporation for example—in the last 2 years in India, the company has undertaken many road and metro projects, with an allocated budget of US$40 million.

TAITRA has taken action to assist Taiwanese construction companies to further develop foreign markets. After taking the business opportunities, ease of doing business, and political stability into consideration, TAITRA has chosen India, Vietnam, and the United States as targets for Taiwanese construction companies to expand their business.

Cultural and Creative Industry

TAITRA actively assists companies with business strengths to enter the international market. With a focus on the Chinese market, TAITRA has taken advantage of Taiwan's sharing the same language and heritage to promote products with strong Taiwanese characteristics, such as National Palace Museum merchandise, Hakka and aboriginal merchandise, and creative daily-life products. In the future, TAITRA aims to promote Chinese culture and creative industry through cooperative endeavors between China and Taiwan. Also, TAITRA is continuing to assist local enterprises in tapping into the Japanese and Southeast Asian markets for online games and animation. China is also a target market to be explored.

However, if these services are as well defined, the TAITRA website is still too focused on general information than on e-promotion and needs to shift its focus more toward e-promotion, B2B (business-to-business) opportunities presented in and trade mission (outgoing more than incoming) programs. These trade promotion services are appreciated by foreign trade missions seeking partners or trade information at the local level.

However, more details are provided by the Taiwan Trade website (http://www.taiwantrade.com.tw) and the Asian Trade Promotion Forum (http://www.atpf.org/www1/html/en/w_chinesetaipei.html).

CASE 9

United States

Trade Promotion Policy

A Look Into U.S. Trade Policy, the External and Institutional Environment, and the U.S. Trade Facilitation Measures

The U.S. trade environment can be illustrated through a series of indicators that provide an overview of the latest trade policy and performance, as well as the U.S. institutional trade environment, prepared by the World Bank team of economists and experts. Such indicators, called Trade-At-A-Glance (TAAG) tables, illustrate U.S. trade policy.

There are key considerations on U.S. Trade Promotion Policy, which can be found in the Government Accountability Office (GAO) Report, December 9, 2009. The report is published and authorized for full reproduction under the following title "Observation on U.S. and Foreign Countries Export Promotion Activities."

GAO Observations on U.S. Export Promotion Activities

Exports, and trade more broadly, contribute to the U.S. economy in a variety of ways. Trade enables the United States to achieve a higher standard of living through producing and exporting goods and services that are produced in the United States relatively efficiently, and importing goods and services that are produced in the United States relatively inefficiently.

Rationales for export promotion programs include macroeconomic considerations such as job creation and economic growth. Others are based on microeconomic considerations such as "market failures" (e.g., where imperfect information prevents markets from generating the most efficient outcome). Rationales also exist for export programs based on achieving broader trade policy objectives, such as helping U.S. exporters overcome foreign trade barriers that make it difficult for U.S. products to penetrate foreign markets. However, measuring the effectiveness of export promotion activities is difficult. For example, quantifying the growth in exports is complicated by the fact that other factors, such as government policies and firm-specific conditions, also determine growth.

Export promotion efforts in the United States are guided by the National Export Strategy. According to the strategy, 20 agencies are part of the Trade Promotion Coordinating Committee (TPCC); 9 of these agencies have budgets for programs or activities related to export promotion, with the Departments of Commerce, Agriculture, and State actively engaged in export promotion overseas. Agency export promotion activities include providing basic export counseling, assisting with collecting and providing data on foreign markets, and advising firms on how to best market their products overseas.

While the GAO has not recently performed an in-depth comparison of U.S. and foreign export promotion activities, the findings and recommendations in the past reviews of U.S. agencies are consistent with expert studies looking at export promotion practices in other countries. Specifically, the GAO has identified elements of U.S. export promotion activities that warrant attention: (1) coordination, (2) targeted services for small and medium-sized enterprises (SMEs) and other priorities, (3) performance monitoring, and (4) partnerships and methodologies for setting user fees. The expert studies reviewed by the GAO echo the importance of each of these elements with regard to the activities of foreign export promotion agencies and may be informative for policy discussions about U.S. export promotion activities.

As Congress considers policies to bolster the recovery of the U.S. economy, it must consider the full range of tools available to stimulate growth and create new jobs, including promoting exports. This case study will provide an overview of (1) the benefits of exporting, rationale for export promotion activities, and an overview of the extent of U.S. activities and (2) observations about U.S. and foreign export promotion, focusing on the importance of coordination, targeting services, performance monitoring, and collaborative partnerships. The GAO has reviewed export promotion activities in several agencies over the years, including the Department of Commerce and the Export-Import Bank, and recommended changes to improve the data and information regarding their export promotion activities. In turn, the agencies have responded to these recommendations. For example, the Department of Commerce agreed with recommendations made earlier this year to improve their procedures for determining costs, setting user fees, and obtaining their information about customers and demand for the export promotion services they offer. Similarly, the Export-Import Bank has taken several steps to respond to GAO recommendations regarding the number of transactions that directly benefit small businesses and their system for estimating the value of direct small-business support for those transactions where the exporter is not known at the time the Export-Import Bank authorizes the transaction.

Remarks about U.S. export promotion efforts are based on a variety of reports and testimonies issued on international trade over the past 4 years and include some additional observations about foreign export promotion practices based on a preliminary review of several key expert studies.

The Benefits of Exporting and U.S. Efforts to Promote Exports

Exports Provide Economic Benefits

Trade, and exports more specifically, contributes to the U.S. economy in a variety of ways. Trade generally enables the United States to achieve a higher standard of living through exporting goods and services that are produced domestically relatively efficiently and importing goods and services that are produced domestically relatively inefficiently. An indication of this is that firms engaged in the international marketplace tend to exhibit higher rates of productivity growth and pay higher wages and benefits to their workers than domestically oriented firms of the same size.

In addition, the benefits of exports accrue to many U.S. states. For example, in 2008, according to the Department of Commerce, Oregon's exports totaled US$19.4 billion, with computers, electronics, and agricultural products accounting for more than half of that amount. According to the Idaho Department of Commerce, in 2008, Idaho exported US$5.01 billion worth of goods, with exports of high-tech products including semiconductors, computers, and capital equipment accounting for 63%, or US$3.2 billion, of the total. Agricultural and food exports from Idaho totaled approximately US$676 million, about 14% of its total exports.

Exports can also serve as a countercyclical force for the U.S. economy, stimulating the U.S. economy when demand from abroad is greater than domestic demand. For several years, the United States increasingly imported more than it exported and served as an engine of growth for other nations. In contrast, when the U.S. economy slowed in 2007 through the first two quarters of 2009, the economic downturn was somewhat mitigated by an improving trade balance. For example, with continued global demand for U.S. goods and services, increases in net exports accounted for over half of U.S. economic growth in 2007 and 2008.

Export Promotion Is Based on Several Rationales

Several rationales exist for the use of government export promotion programs to support exporting firms and sectors. In addition to macroeconomic considerations of job creation and economic growth, microeconomic considerations exist for government programs to address "market failures"—where conditions such as imperfect information and entry barriers prevent markets from generating the most efficient outcome. Rationales may also exist for export programs based on achieving broader trade policy objectives, such as helping U.S.

exporters overcome foreign trade barriers that make it difficult for U.S. products to penetrate foreign markets. Examples of export promotion addressing market failures and achieving broader trade policy objectives include the following:

- *Foreign market information.* Some firms may not export because they lack information about export markets, but U.S. officials abroad may have access to commercially valuable information about foreign markets that the private sector may not otherwise be able to access.
- *Advocacy.* Government representation on behalf of a firm competing for a potential export sale may influence procurement decisions, particularly in helping establish a firm's credibility in foreign markets.
- *Export finance assistance.* Government finance can fill gaps created when the private sector is reluctant to finance certain exports, particularly for SMEs.

Not withstanding these rationales, measuring the effectiveness of export promotion activities is inherently difficult. For example, quantifying the growth in exports is complicated by the fact that other factors, such as government policies and firm-specific conditions, also determine growth. Nevertheless, according to the World Bank, the number of national export promotion agencies worldwide has tripled over the past 2 decades.

U.S. Export Promotion Is Supported by a Wide Variety of Agencies and Activities

Export promotion efforts in the United States are guided by the National Export Strategy and are pursued by a wide variety of agencies and through a wide range of activities. According to the strategy, 20 export promotion agencies are part of the TPCC, of which 9 have budgets for programs or activities related to export promotion, with the Department of Commerce, the Department of Agriculture, and the Department of State actively engaged in export promotion overseas.

To support U.S. businesses domestically, as well as gather data and information about local markets, the Department of Agriculture has 101 offices in 81 countries and the Department of Commerce has 126 offices in more than 80 countries. State personnel provide in-country services at approximately 100 embassies overseas where either the Department of Commerce or the Department of Agriculture lacks a presence. In both 2007 and 2008, the budget for U.S. trade promotion activities was about US$1.3 billion. In 2009, TPCC agencies requested US$1.2 billion in funding, with the Department of Agriculture, the Department of Commerce, and the Department of State accounting for 91% of the total trade promotion budget authority.

The wide range of activities that are considered export promotion include

- providing basic export counseling,
- assisting with collecting and providing data on foreign markets,
- advising firms on how to best market their products overseas,
- providing loans, insurance, and guarantee programs,
- advocating on behalf of domestic firms, and
- monitoring trade agreements.

While the GAO has not recently performed an in-depth comparison of U.S. and foreign export promotion activities, the findings and recommendations in the past reviews of U.S. agencies are consistent with expert studies looking at export promotion practices in other countries. Specifically, the GAO has identified elements of U.S. export promotion activities that warrant attention: (1) coordination, (2) targeted services for SMEs and other priorities, (3) performance monitoring, and (4) partnerships and methodologies for setting user fees. The expert studies reviewed by the GAO echo the importance of each of these elements with regard to the activities of foreign export promotion agencies and may be informative for policy discussions about U.S. export promotion activities. The GAO has begun a new body of work in this area based on renewed congressional interest.

Coordination of U.S. Export Promotion Activities

U.S. export promotion activities are coordinated by the TPCC. To address a longstanding congressional concern over a lack of effective coordination, the GAO has reviewed the TPCC several times since its inception. In 2006, the GAO testified that the TPCC had made progress over time in improving coordination, including interagency training and joint outreach.

However, in both 2006 and 2009, the GAO found the TPCC continued to face challenges in other areas of its coordination responsibilities.

For example, in March 2009, the GAO testified that the National Export Strategy continues to lack an overall review of agencies' allocation of resources relative to government-wide export promotion priorities. Similarly, the GAO testified in 2006 that, despite its mandate to propose a unified federal trade promotion budget, the TPCC continued to have little influence over agencies' allocation of resources for trade promotion.

Observations about the importance of clearly coordinated responsibilities among export promotion agencies are consistent with findings in several expert studies that examined foreign export promotion practices. For example, the International Trade Centre (ITC) reported that most successful exporting countries have established a central or national export promotion agency that coordinates implementation of the national export strategy, leads in creation of a support network, and acts as a first stop for the business community.

In a review of 104 countries, the World Bank study found that a single and strong export promotion agency is preferred to the sometimes observed proliferation of agencies within countries. Well-coordinated activities among a larger partnership of support agencies are emphasized in studies by the Australian Trade Authority (Austrade) and the Boston Consulting Group. Austrade, for example, stated that effectively coordinating export service providers is important for potential and new-to-export firms, since some—especially SMEs—have encountered difficulties in identifying or accessing appropriate services for their needs.

Examples of notable foreign coordination efforts that the reports cited include:

- Canada's National Sector Teams and Regional Trade Networks that were created to enhance coordination and improve access to services for the business community
- The Philippine Export Act that gave an apex body, the Export Development Council, overall responsibility for formulating and coordinating the national export development effort. The council was chaired by the Secretary of the Department of Trade and Industry and had cabinet-level members from the eight ministries concerned with economic development.

Targeting Services for SMEs and Other Priorities

Providing services targeted to small businesses has been a high priority for U.S. export promotion activities. The Department of Commerce seeks to broaden and deepen the exporter base with the majority of exports supported by its commercial service deriving from SMEs while for the U.S. Export-Import Bank, Congress requires that a certain percentage of financing be for small business. The GAO has found limitations in both programs. In 2009, the GAO recommended that the Department of Commerce take steps to improve its databases and procedures because they lacked reliable information about the size, location, and type of its customers. In 2006, the GAO recommended, among other things, that the Export-Import Bank more accurately determine the number of transactions that directly benefit small business and improve the system for estimating the value of direct small-business support for those transactions where the exporter is not known at the time Export-Import Bank authorizes the transaction. As the GAO testified in 2008, the Export-Import Bank has taken several steps in response to those recommendations.

The GAO's observations about the importance of targeting services, for example, to SMEs and other assistance priorities are reflected in expert studies on foreign export promotion. For example, most of the studies the GAO reviewed recognized that SMEs have unique needs and that services should be tailored to account for common financing and informational constraints faced by smaller firms. Several studies also emphasized the importance of prioritizing assistance to certain sectors or firms based on the exporting goals of each country. According to the Boston Consulting Group, fragmentation of efforts from having too many targets tends to undermine an agency's chance of success. As a result, it suggested screening for export-ready firms and transitioning firms across different states of exporting, focusing on services for smaller firms that are "threshold" or "mature" exporters. Conversely, the World Bank emphasized prioritizing assistance to large firms that are not yet exporters, and both the World Bank and the Asia Pacific Economic Cooperation studies discussed a focus on nontraditional export sectors. To select priorities, Nathan Associates explained that sectors, markets, or firms should be selected on the basis of market research combined with stakeholder consultation. Examples of targeted or tailored foreign promotion efforts that the studies cited include the following:

- The UK's Export Explorer and Passport to Export Success programs that were targeted to new exporters. Export Explorer, for instance, combined coaching at home with support from the overseas network, giving new exporters the experience of exporting to geographically close markets and enabling them to gain confidence.
- The Indian Ministry of Industry's cluster-development program and Malaysian efforts to connect SMEs with other exporters. Malaysia's Small and Medium Industries Development Corporation, for instance, linked SMEs into the supply chain of larger multinational corporations that have the systems and knowledge needed for SMEs to become globally competitive.

Performance Monitoring

While recognizing the challenge of measuring the effectiveness of export promotion activities, the GAO has found in several reviews of

U.S. programs that performance monitoring could be improved. For a number of years the GAO has noted that TPCC agencies do not identify or measure agencies' progress toward mutual goals as part of the National Export Strategy. More recently, in March 2009, the GAO reported that better evaluation by the Department of Commerce of its commercial service fee-based programs and customers, including states, could improve program continuity, help managers target their resources more efficiently and effectively, assess costs and benefits, and help Congress make more informed funding decisions. In 2008, the GAO reported that the Export-Import Bank had developed performance standards for its small business financing in most, although not all, of the areas specified by Congress, that some measures for monitoring progress against the standards lacked targets and timeframes, and that the Export-Import Bank was just beginning to compile and use the small business information it was collecting to improve operations. The GAO recommended that the Export-Import Bank establish performance standards for functions not currently addressed, revise several current measures to include measurable targets and time frames, and take steps to establish a measure for financing for small businesses owned by socially and economically disadvantaged individuals and women.

Using meaningful performance monitoring as a learning tool is also discussed in the expert studies on foreign export promotion. The ITC's executive forum noted that, although performance evaluation is inherently challenging, without widely accepted performance measures, export promotion agencies have difficulty forming and implementing export strategies. The center outlined measurements that focus on the impact of export promotion agency services rather than export quantities. Similarly, the Boston Consulting Group stated that evaluation is needed to justify and account for the use of public monies and to obtain feedback for the allocation of resources and the design of programs. To achieve these goals, export promotion agencies may use a collection of quantitative and qualitative measures combined with independent feedback from clients. Nathan Associates also emphasized the role that assessing client satisfaction plays in program design but suggested that client satisfaction be assessed through in-depth interviews rather than surveys that may be biased. Examples of foreign efforts to improve performance monitoring that the studies cited include the following:

- Australia's use of a Customer Relationship Management (CRM) System in order to track export results, assess client satisfaction, and obtain lessons learned. Australia collected this information as part of its fee-based services system and each of its three trade-related outcomes—awareness raising, export services, and export finance assistance—was assigned a target against which results were measured.
- New Zealand's performance evaluation system that empha-sized client input by compiling monthly feedback gathered by account managers, verifying every 6 months by inde-pendent survey and concentrating on achieving a high deliver-in-full-and-on-time rating for specific services.

Partnerships to Improve Export Promotion Efforts

Recognizing the value of partnerships, U.S. export promotion agencies have developed collaborative relationships with the private sector, cit-ies, and states. For example, the Department of Commerce initiated its Corporate Partnership Program, leveraging the private sector's sales and marketing expertise in 2004. Likewise, the Department of Agriculture has programs that work in partnership with the private sector includ-ing the Market Access Program and the Foreign Market Development Program. The GAO has evaluated federal-state partnerships but has not evaluated private sector partnerships. For example, the GAO reported in 2009 that state offices often partner with the Department of Commerce on trade missions and other activities, and most states responding to a GAO survey reported that the Department of Commerce's services were important to their export promotion capabilities.

A third of the states also said they provide grants or payments to defray firms' costs and to facilitate access to Department of Commerce programs. More generally, in 2006, the GAO testified that based on their long record of oversight, the TPCC could continue to make improvements in outreach efforts to the private sector and that sustained high-level administration involvement would be necessary for the TPCC to achieve its fundamental objectives.

To ensure costs charged for export promotion services are appropriate, the GAO has also recently done work related to cost recovery for some Department of Commerce programs. In 2009, the GAO reviewed the Department of Commerce's methodology for establishing fees for export promotion services.

While the Department of Commerce collects about US$10 million annually through fees, the GAO found that it lacked good information on the true costs of providing services. Similarly, the Department of Commerce lacked reliable information about how its fees (or lack thereof) affected their customers' access to the program, or how they compared to state or private sector fees. As a result, it was unclear whether the fees the Department of Commerce established reflect their policy objectives or whether they optimize the efficient and effective management of these programs. The GAO recommended that the Department of Commerce improve its procedures for setting user fees and collect and process more reliable information about its customers. More broadly, the importance of both public and private sector involvement—as well as appropriately set user fees—is another key observation discussed in the expert studies. Regarding the role of contributions from the private sector, several studies discussed the importance of including private sector methodologies and input to ensure firm needs do not outgrow the expertise of the export assistance offered. These studies also addressed the importance of independence, to guarantee continuity as governments change and the autonomy needed to operate by commercial principles. For example, the World Bank study found that export promotion agencies with a large share of the executive board in the hands of the private sector, but with a large share of public sector funding, are most effective. Studies by Nathan Associates and the ITC also emphasized the importance of a predictable and long-term level of public sector funding, with fees charged for some services.

Specific examples of how foreign export agencies charge fees or incorporate public and private sector involvement that the reports cited include the following:

- The Danish Trade Council and Enterprise Ireland, whose executive boards were composed mostly of successful business people representing key sectors in the economy
- Costa Rica's semiprivate trade promotion agency that was run by a mostly private board of directors but was supported by a statutorily independent source of income from taxes in the free trade zones
- Australia's system of providing free services to help "intenders" and "new exporters" build export readiness, select target markets, and obtain initial market information while customized services that helped companies understand and enter new export markets were billed on a full cost-recovery basis

Conclusion

The role that exports can play in the U.S. economy, as well as the role of U.S. agencies in developing and implementing national export promotion programs, is well described by the GAO, and this institution can be praised for its transparency. In fact there are no other countries that have such evaluation programs implemented on a regular basis and publishing their findings and conclusions in the public place.

International Trade Organizations and National Trade Promotion Organizations on the Web

International Trade Organizations	United Nations Conference on Trade and Development (UNCTAD): http://www.unctad.org
	UNCTAD Tradepoint Development Center: http://www.untpdc.org
	World Trade Center Association (WTCA): http://www.wtca.org
	World Trade Organization (WTO): http://www.wto.org
	International Trade Centre (ITC): http://www.intracen.org
Australia	Austrade (The Australian Trade Commission): http://www.austrade.gov.au
Canada	Department of Foreign Affairs and International Trade (DFAIT): http://www.international.gc.ca/international/index.aspx?view=d
China	Ministry of Foreign Trade and Economic Cooperation (MOFTEC): http://english.mofcom.gov.cn
Ecuador	The Export and Investment Promotion Corporation (CORPEI): http://www.corpei.org
France	Ubifrance: http://www.ubifrance.fr
Greece	Hellenic Foreign Trade Board (HEPO): http://www.hepo.gr/?lang_chosen=en&lang_choosen=en
Hong Kong	Hong Kong Trade Development Council (HKTDC): http://www.hktdc.com
Iceland	Trade Council of Iceland: http://www.icetrade.is
Indonesia	The Ministry of Industry and Trade (INDAG): http://www.depperindag.tripod.com/eng_2000/p
Japan	Japan External Trade Organization (JETRO): http://www.jetro.go.jp/

Korea	Korea Trade Investment Promotion Agency (KOTRA): http://english.kotra.or.kr
Malaysia	Malaysia External Trade Development Corporation (MA-TRADE): http://www.matrade.gov.my
Malta	Malta External Trade Corporation (METCO): http://malta enterprise.com
New Zealand	New Zealand Trade Development Board: http://www.tradenz.govt.nz
Oman	The Omani Centre for Investment Promotion and Export Development (OCIPED): http://www.ociped.com
Philippines	Department of Trade and Industry (DTI): http://www.dti.gov.ph
Romania	Romanian Center for Trade and Investment: http://www.romtradeinvest.ro/
Singapore	Singapore Trade Development Board (STDB), now IE Singapore: http://www.iesingapore.com
Sweden	Swedish Trade Council: http://www.swedishtrade.se
Taiwan	Taiwan External Trade Development Council (TAITRA): http://www.taitra.org.tw
Thailand	Department of Export Promotion (DEP): http://www.thaitrade.com
United Kingdom	UK Trade and Investment: http://www.ukti.gov.uk
United States	International Trade Administration (ITA): http://www.ita.doc.gov

Notes

Introduction

1. Czinkota (1983).

Chapter 2

1. Cegli and Dini (1999). For ordering information, see El Pinolero's Nicaragua website (http://ni.irias.biz/hamacasNY.html).
2. Kotabe and Czinkota (1992).
3. Cegli and Dini (1999).

Chapter 3

1. See "Taipei world trade center," Asian Trade Promotion Forum, http://www.atpf.org/www1/html/en/w_chinesetaipei.html
2. Hibbert (1990).
3. World Bank (2001).

Chapter 4

1. Porter (1998); Porter (2008).
2. Porter (2008).
3. Porter (2008).
4. Porter (1998); Porter (2008).

Chapter 5

1. "Report of the Commonwealth Committee on Terrorism (CCT): Commonwealth Plan of Action," http://www.thecommonwealth.org/Templates/Internal.asp?NodeID=35145
2. World Economic Forum (2010), p. 9.
3. World Economic Forum (2010), p. 5.
4. World Economic Forum (2010), p. 9.

Chapter 6

1. World Bank (2004).

Chapter 7

1. See also Orellana (2008).

Chapter 8

1. Australian Trade Commission (2001).

2. *Canada's State of Trade: Trade and Investment Update 2010*, http://www
.international.gc.ca/economist-economiste/performance/state-point/state_2010
_point/2010_7.aspx?lang=eng&view=d

Chapter 9

1. Martincus (2008).
2. Yager (2009).
3. Biesebroeck (2010).
4. Yager (2009).

Chapter 10

1. This chapter makes reference to Belisle (2000).
2. Belisle (2000).
3. Belisle (2000), p. 34.

Case 1

1. Badrinath and Wignaraja (2004).

2. "Trade Map: Trade Statistics for International Business Development,"
http://www.trademap.org

3. "Trade Map: Trade Statistics for International Business Development,"
http://www.trademap.org

4. International Trade Centre UNCTAD/WTO (2007).

5. International Trade Centre UNCTAD/WTO (2007).

6. "Guided Tour and User Guide," http://www.investmentmap.org/guided
_tour.aspx

7. Market Access Map (2006).

8. Market Access Map (2006).

9. Market Access Map (2006).

10. Market Access Map (2006).

Case 2

1. "Statistics Database," http://stat.wto.org/Home/WSDBHome.aspx?Language =E

2. "Foreign Direct Investment (FDI) Confidence Index," http://www .atkearney.com/index.php/Publications/foreign-direct-investment-confidence -index.html

Case 3

1. UK Trade & Investment (2010).

2. UK Trade & Investment (2010).

3. UK Trade & Investment (2010).

4. UK Trade & Investment (2010).

5. UK Trade & Investment (2010).

6. UK Trade & Investment (2011).

Case 4

1. "Market: Fair Trade Cotton Market," http://unctad.org/infocomm/anglais/ cotton/market.htm#fair

2. "Market: Fair Trade Cotton Market," http://unctad.org/infocomm/anglais/ cotton/market.htm#fair

3. "Facts & Figures," http://www.fta.org.au/about-fairtrade/facts-figures

4. Fairtrade Labelling Organizations International (2009).

Case 6

1. "Exporters," http://www.gov.mb.ca/trade/export/links/ex_exsrce.html

2. DeJong (2010).

3. DeJong (2010).

4. "Market Reports," http://www.tradecommissioner.gc.ca/eng/market-report -access.jsp

5. "10 Steps to Successful Exporting," http://sbinfocanada.about.com/od/ canadaexport/a/10exportsteps.htm

6. "ExportAssistance,"http://www.york.ca/Business/Export+Assistance.htm ?ODA=1

7. *Speaking Globally: An Exporter's Guide to Effective Presentations*, http:// publications.gc.ca/site/eng/254536/publication.html

8. "New Exporters to Border States (NEBS)/Export USA Program," http://www .buffaloniagara.org/Events/NewExporterstoBorderStatesNEBSExportUSAProgram

9. "Market Reports—by Industry Sectors," http://www.tradecommissioner .gc.ca/eng/market-reports-sectors.jsp

10. "Doing Business With Canada," http://www.canadainternational.gc.ca/ ci-ci/commerce_canada/index.aspx?view=d

11. "Evaluation of the International Business Opportunities Centre (IBOC)," http://www.international.gc.ca/about-a_propos/oig-big/2004/evaluation/ IBOC-COAI.aspx?lang=eng&view=d

Case 7

1. "Mauritius Data," http://data.worldbank.org/country/mauritius

Case 8

1. "TWTC Nangang Exhibition Hall," http://www.twtcnangang.com/?Lang =en-US

References

Ali, M. Y. (1998). Managers' perceived barriers to export: A study of rural Australian small and medium-sized enterprises. In G. Brandon (Ed.), *Proceedings of the Australia and New Zealand Marketing Academy Conference* (pp. 28–41). Dunedin, New Zealand: University of Otago.

Ali, M. Y. (2000). Export promotion programs and export performance: A study of SME managers' awareness and usage of export promotion programs. In P. Enderwick & E. Rose (Eds.), *Proceedings of the Australia and New Zealand International Business Academy Conference* (pp. 1–10). Auckland, New Zealand: University of Auckland.

A. T. Kearney. (n.d.). Foreign direct investment (FDI) confidence index. Retrieved from http://www.atkearney.com/index.php/Publications/foreign-direct-investment-confidence-index.html

Australian Trade Commission (2001). *Knowing and growing the exporter community.* Sydney: Austrade.

Badrinath, R., & Wignaraja, G. (2004). Building business competitiveness. *International Trade Forum, 2.* Retrieved from http://www.tradeforum.org/news/fullstory.php/aid/676

Belisle, J. D. (2000). Redefining trade promotion: Messages for TPOs. *International Trade Centre* (4), p. 4. Paper presented on ITC's Executive Forum on National Export Strategies—International Trade Forum held in Marrakech, Morocco, Geneva.

Biesebroeck, J. V., et al. (2010, April). *The impact of trade promotion services on Canadian exporter performance* (discussion paper). Retrieved from http://www.econ.kuleuven.be/eng/ew/discussionpapers/Dps10/Dps1f014.pdf

Buffalo Niagara Enterprise. (n.d.). New exporters to border states (NEBS)/export USA program. Retrieved from http://www.buffaloniagara.org/Events/NewExporterstoBorderStatesNEBSExportUSAProgram

Canada's International Gateway. (n.d.). Doing business with Canada. Retrieved from http://www.canadainternational.gc.ca/ci-ci/commerce_canada/index.aspx?view=d

Canada's International Gateway. (n.d.). Evaluation of the International Business Opportunities Centre (IBOC). Retrieved from http://www.international.gc.ca/about-a_propos/oig-big/2004/evaluation/IBOC-COAI.aspx?lang=eng&view=d

Cavusgil, S. T. (1990). Export development efforts in the United States: Experiences and lessons learned. In S. T. Cavusgil & M. R. Czinkota (Eds.), *International perspectives on trade promotion and assistance* (pp. 173–183). New York, NY: Quorum Books.

Cegli, G., & Dini, M. (1999). SME cluster and network development in developing countries: The experience of UNIDO. *United Nations Industrial Development Organization.* Retrieved from http://unido.org/fileadmin/import/userfiles/russof/giopaper.pdf

Commonwealth Secretariat. (n.d.). Report of the Commonwealth Committee on Terrorism (CCT): Commonwealth plan of action. Retrieved from http://www.thecommonwealth.org/Templates/Internal.asp?NodeID=35145

Crick, D., & Czinkota, M. R. (1995). Export assistance: Another look at whether we are supporting the best programmes. *International Marketing Review, 12*(3), 61–72.

Czinkota, M. ed. (1983). *Export promotion: The public and private sector interaction.* New York, NY: Praeger.

Czinkota, M. (2001). *Best practices in international business* (with I. Ronkainen). Fort Worth, TX: Harcourt, 2001.

Czinkota, M. (2002). Export promotion: A framework for finding opportunity in change. *Thunderbird International Business Review, 44*(3), 315.

Czinkota, M. (2009). International business: Fundamentals of international business (2nd ed.; with I. Ronkainen & M. Moffett). New York, NY: Wessex.

Czinkota, M. (2010). *Emerging trends, threats, and opportunities in international marketing: What executives need to know* (with M. Kotabe & I. Ronkainen). New York, NY: Business Expert Press.

Czinkota, M. (2010). *International business* (8th ed.; with I. Ronkainen & M. Moffett). Hoboken, NJ: Wiley.

Czinkota, M. (2010). *International marketing* (9th ed.; with I. Ronkainen). Cincinnati, OH: Cengage.

Czinkota, M. (2011). *The future of global business* (with I. Ronkainen & M. Kotabe). London, UK: Routledge.

DeJong, C. (2010). *Linking in to global value chains: A guide for small and medium-sized enterprises.* Foreign Affairs and International Trade Canada. Retrieved from http://www.international.gc.ca/tcs-sdc/assets/pdfs/gvc_guide_cvm-eng.pdf

Dichtl, E., Koeglmayr, H. G., & Muller, S. (1990). International orientation as a precondition for export success. *Journal of International Business Studies, 21*(1), 23–40.

Gencturk, E., & Kotabe, M. (2001). The effect of export assistance program usage on export performance: A contingency explanation. *Journal of International Marketing, 9*(2), 51–72.

Fair Trade Association. (n.d.). Facts & figures. Retrieved from http://www.fta
.org.au/about-fairtrade/facts-figures

Fairtrade Labelling Organizations International. (2009). *Growing stronger together.*
Annual Report 2009–10. Retrieved from http://www.fairtrade.net/fileadmin/
user_upload/content/2009/resources/FLO_Annual-Report-2009_komplett
_double_web.pdf

Foreign Affairs and International Trade Canada. (n.d.). *Canada's state of trade: Trade*
and investment update 2010. Retrieved from http://www.international.gc.ca/
economist-economiste/performance/state-point/state_2010_point/2010_7
.aspx?lang=eng&view=d

Foreign Affairs and International Trade. (n.d.). Market reports. Retrieved from
http://www.tradecommissioner.gc.ca/eng/market-report-access.jsp

Foreign Affairs and International Trade. (n.d.). Market reports—by industry sectors.
Retrieved from http://www.tradecommissioner.gc.ca/eng/market-report-access
.jsp

Hibbert, E. P. (1990). *The management of international trade promotion.* New
York, NY: Routledge.

InfoComm. (n.d.). Market: Fair trade cotton market. Retrieved from United
Nations Conference on Trade and Development website http://unctad.org/
infocomm/anglais/cotton/market.htm#fair

International Trade Centre. (n.d.). Guided tour and user guide. Retrieved from
International Trade Centre website, http://www.investmentmap.org/guided
_tour.aspx

International Trade Centre. (n.d.). Trade map: Trade statistics for international
business development. Retrieved from International Trade Centre website,
http://www.trademap.org

International Trade Centre UNCTAD/WTO. (2007, May). *Investment map user*
guide. Retrieved from http://www.investmentmap.org/docs/invmap-userguide
-en.pdf

Katsikeas, C. S., & Morgan, R. E. (1994). Differences in perceptions of exporting problems based on firm size and export market experience. *European*
Journal of Marketing, 28(5), 17–35.

Kotabe, M., & Czinkota, M. (1992). State government promotion of manufacturing exports: A gap analysis. *Journal of International Business Studies, 23*(4),
637–658.

Kroll (2006, February 14). Trade promotion best practices. *Kroll Tendencias.*
Retrieved from http://www.infoamericas.com

Leonidou, L. C. (2004). An analysis of the barriers hindering small business
export development. *Journal of Small Business Management, 42*(3), 279–302.

Manitoba Trade and Investments. (n.d.). Exporters. Retrieved from http://www
.gov.mb.ca/trade/export/links/ex_exsrce.html

Market Access Map. (2006, December) *Market Access Map—user guide: Making tariffs and market barriers transparent.* Retrieved from http://www.macmap .org/User.Guide.aspx

Martincus, C. V. (2008, October 13). *Is export promotion effective in Latin America and the Caribbean?.* Paper presented at the Seventh World Conference of Trade Promotion Organizations, The Hague, The Netherlands. Survey retrieved from http://www.iadb.org/research/books/idb-bk-100/ppt/thehague.pdf

Masaaki, K. (1998). Efficiency vs. effectiveness orientation of global sourcing strategy: A comparison of U.S. and Japanese multinational companies. *Academy of Management Executive, 12*(November), 107–119.

Moini, A. H. (1998). Small firms exporting: How effective are government export assistance programs? *Journal of Small Business Management, 36*(1), 1–15.

Morgan, R. E. (1997). Export stimuli and export barriers: Evidence from empirical research studies. *European Business Review, 97*(2), 68–79.

Orellana, E. (2008, June). The weak link in trade promotion: SMEs and export-oriented clusters. *Kroll Tendencias, 75.* Retrieved from http://krolltendencias .com/site/index.php?option=com_user&view=login&return=aHR0 cDovL2tyb2xsdGVuZGVuY2lhcy5jb20vc2l0ZS9pcm93c2UtYXJjaGl2 ZXMvdHJhZGGUtY29tcGV0aXRpdmVuZXNzLWFuZC1pbnZlc3 RtZW50LzE0MC10aGUtd2Vhay1saW5rLWluLXRyYWRlLXByb 21vdGlvbi1zbWVzLWFuZC1leHBvcnQtb3JpZW50ZWQtY2xc 3RlcnMuaHRtbA==

Porter, M. (1998). *The competitive advantage of nations.* New York: Free Press.

Porter, M. (2008). *On competition. Harvard Business Review* (Boston, MA: Harvard Business School).

Ramaseshan, B., & Souter, G. N. (1996). Combined effects of incentives and barriers on firms' export decisions. *International Business Review, 5*(1), 53–66.

Regional Municipality of York. (n.d.). Export assistance. Retrieved from http:// www.york.ca/Business/Export+Assistance.htm?ODA=1

Salomon, R. M., & Shaver, J. M. (2005). Learning by exporting: New insights from examining firm innovation. *Journal of Economics and Management Strategy, 14*(2), 431–460.

Seringhaus, F., & Botschen, G. (1991). Cross-national comparison of export promotion services: The view of Canadian and Austrian companies. *Journal of International Business Studies, 22*(1), 115–134.

Seringhaus, F., & Rosson, P. (1990). *Government export promotion: The global perspective.* London: Routledge.

Shamsuddoha, A. K., & Ali, M. Y. (2006). Mediated effects of export promotion programs on firm export performance. *Asia Pacific Journal of Marketing and Logistics, 18*(2), 93–110.

Team Canada. (n.d.). *Speaking globally: An exporter's guide to effective presentations.* Retrieved from http://publications.gc.ca/site/eng/254536/publication.html

Team Canada. (n.d.). 10 steps to successful exporting. Retrieved from About web-site, http://sbinfocanada.about.com/od/canadaexport/a/10exportsteps.htm

UK Trade & Investment. (2010, October 13–15). *Following up with clients to ensure impact.* Paper presented at the Eighth TPO Network World Conference and Awards, Mexico City, Mexico. PowerPoint slides retrieved from http://docs.google.com/viewer?a=v&q=cache:a6PsWzIloIMJ:www.tponetwork.net/Conference%2520Documents/8th%2520Conference%2520Documents/Speakers%2520-%2520speaches/UKTI_Following%2520up%2520with%2520clients.pdf+Sound+understanding+of+service+quality+strengths+and+weaknesses+and+how+they+affect+impact.&hl=en&gl=us&pid=bl&srcid=ADGEESiznaGUYFkxJCuFFXDmKsZwhLAvHm11iBHnU6XNHzgcL05xz6jaY2YkGvLBUksLs0glC7Q4lE_iElyOj6w0voFcZdE6CjbLaNpkP3wjmUGearCxgq73ncO9cPlkzSHfLUuGJOUJ&sig=AHIEtbRDpBi4wK_vfYYv6d0nmrIzAExI0w&pli=1

UK Trade & Investment. (2011, October 3). Passport to export. Retrieved from http://www.ukti.gov.uk/fr_fr/export/howwehelp/passporttoexport.html

Wilkinson, T. J. (2006). Entrepreneurial climate and the U.S. foreign offices as predictors of export success. *Journal of Small Business Management, 44*(1), 99–113.

World Bank. (2001). Why have trade promotion organizations failed, and how they can be revitalized? *PREM Notes, 56*(August), 1–4.

World Bank. (n.d.). Mauritius data. Retrieved from http://data.worldbank.org/country/mauritius

World Bank. (2004). *Global economic prospects 2004: Realizing the development promise of the Doha Agenda.* Washington, DC: World Bank.

World Economic Forum. (2010). Fostering recovery by facilitating trade: The enabling trade index 2010. In R. Z. Lawrence, et al. (Eds.), *The global enabling trade report* (pp. 5, 9). Geneva, Switzerland: World Economic Forum. Retrieved from http://www3.weforum.org/docs/WEF_GlobalEnablingTrade_Report_2010.pdf

World Trade Organization (WTO). (n.d.). Statistics database. Retrieved July 2, 2010, from http://stat.wto.org/Home/WSDBHome.aspx?Language=E

Yager, L. (2009, December 9). International trade Observations on U.S. and foreign countries' export promotion activities. United States Government Accountability Office. Retrieved from http://www.gao.gov/new.items/d10310t.pdf

Index

Announcing the Business Expert Press Digital Library

Concise E-books Business Students
Need for Classroom and Research

This book can also be purchased in an e-book collection by your library as

- a one-time purchase,
- that is owned forever,
- allows for simultaneous readers,
- has no restrictions on printing,
- can be downloaded as PDFs from within the library community.

Our digital library collections are a great solution to beat the rising cost of textbooks. E-books can be loaded into their course management systems or onto students' e-book readers.

The **Business Expert Press** digital libraries are very affordable, with no obligation to buy in future years.

For more information, please visit **www.businessexpertpress.com/librarians**. To set up a trial in the United States, please contact **Sheri Dean** at sheri.dean@globalepress.com; for all other regions, contact **Nicole Lee** at nicole.lee@igroupnet.com.

OTHER TITLES IN OUR INTERNATIONAL BUSINESS COLLECTION
Series Editors: **S. Tamer Cavusgil**, *Georgia State;* **Michael Czinkota**, *Georgetown;* **Gary Knight**, *Florida State University*

- Conducting Market Research for International Business by S. Tamer Cavusgil, John Riesenberger, and Attila Yaprak
- Export Marketing Strategy: Tactics and Skills That Work by Shaoming Zou, S. Tamer Cavusgil, and Daekwan Kim
- Born Global Firms: A New International Enterprise by S. Tamer Cavusgil and Gary Knight
- The Internationalists: Masters of the Global Game by Catherine W. Scherer
- Doing Business in the ASEAN Countries by Balbir Bhasin

www.ingramcontent.com/pod-product-compliance
Lightning Source LLC
LaVergne TN
LVHW011250200326
834410LV00006B/179